HISTORIC ARCHITECTURE IN THE CARIBBEAN ISLANDS

HISTORIC
ARCHITECTURE IN THE
CARIBBEAN ISLANDS

EDWARD E. CRAIN

UNIVERSITY PRESS OF FLORIDA
GAINESVILLE/TALLAHASSEE/TAMPA/BOCA RATON/PENSACOLA/ORLANDO/MIAMI/JACKSONVILLE

99 98 97 96 95 94 6 5 4 3 2 1

Library of Congress Cataloging-in-Publication Data
Crain, Edward E.
    Historic architecture in the Caribbean Islands / Edward E. Crain
       p.   cm.
    Includes bibliographical references and index.
    ISBN 0-8130-1293-7
    1. Architecture—West Indies.   2. Historic buildings—West Indies.
  I. Title.
  NA791.C73   1994
  720'.9729—dc20   94–3870
                                                   CIP

The University Press of Florida is the scholarly publishing agency for the State University System of Florida, comprised of Florida A & M University, Florida Atlantic University, Florida International University, Florida State University, University of Central Florida, University of Florida, University of North Florida, University of South Florida, and University of West Florida.

University Press of Florida
15 Northwest 15th Street
Gainesville, FL 32611

To the
students at
the Caribbean
School of
Architecture
in Kingston,
Jamaica

CONTENTS

PREFACE

A number of books have been written about the architecture of various individual Caribbean islands, some in considerable detail. What has not been previously accomplished is to put within one cover a well-illustrated work that describes the significant historic architecture of this entire area. That is the goal of this book.

Because of the difficulty of covering so vast a subject area, certain limitations have been imposed. I have included only those islands whose buildings are considered to be of greatest architectural and historic value. (It should be noted that the Bahamas, although not located in the Caribbean, have been included because they are an important part of the West Indies and share an architectural heritage with the islands of the Caribbean.)

I have not tried to cover each island in detail. Sometimes the buildings discussed are from a single major town, usually the capital of the island. I have always tried to choose examples that represent the general architecture on the island.

There is also a time-span limitation. Examples are restricted to buildings constructed before World War II.

I also explore factors that influence architectural development: physical land characteristics, climate, the early Amerindian occupants, the arrival of explorers, the military struggle for control of the islands, immigration from Europe and Africa, emancipation, and immigration from Asia.

I have grouped architectural examples and presented them by building types—residences, military facilities, public and institutional buildings, religious buildings, and miscellaneous buildings.

Because the most apparent architectural influences are those imposed by European powers, I have grouped the islands according to the European power that exerted the most significant influences. In each chapter, English islands are investigated first. These include Jamaica, St. Kitts, Antigua, St. Lucia, Barbados, Grenada, Trinidad, and the Bahamas. Spanish islands include Puerto Rico, Cuba, and the Dominican Republic. French islands include Haiti, Martinique, Guadeloupe, and St. Martin. Dutch islands include Sint Maarten and Curaçao. Danish influence is unique to the U.S. Virgin Islands, formerly the Danish West Indies. To facilitate easy reference for the reader, I maintain this order of presentation, by islands, in each chapter.

INTRODUCTION

The Caribbean Sea, covering an area of approximately 750,000 square miles, is named for the Carib Indians, who once inhabited this area. There are thirty-some major islands and island groups and hundreds of smaller ones, many of them uninhabited. The sea is bounded on the west by the Yucatan Peninsula, Belize, Honduras, Guatemala, and Costa Rica. On the south, the boundary is defined by the coastlines of Panama, Colombia, and Venezuela. On the north, the Caribbean is separated from the Gulf of Mexico and the Atlantic by the Greater Antilles (Cuba, Hispaniola, and Puerto Rico) and the Virgin Islands. The curve of the small islands in the Lesser Antilles defines the eastern boundary.

The Lesser Antilles also have geographical subdivisions that have been named. The Leeward Islands, those lying north of fifteen degrees north latitude, include St. Martin/Sint Maarten, St. Kitts and Nevis, Antigua, Montserrat, Guadeloupe, and Dominica. The Windward Islands, those to the south, include Martinique, St. Lucia, St. Vincent, and Grenada and the Grenadines. The latter list may also include Barbados and Trinidad/Tobago. (In the *political* subdivision used in the British West Indies, Dominica was included in the Windward, not the Leeward Islands.) The Netherlands Antilles (Aruba, Curaçao, and Bonaire) are located just off the coast of northwest Venezuela.

Several maps from the fifteenth century showed a land named Antillia, located far west of Portugal between the Canary Islands and the southeast coast of Asia. Sometimes it was represented as an archipelago, sometimes as a single mass of land. The name *Antilles* was derived from Columbus's belief that he had reached the fabled land of Antillia.

The term *West Indies,* of course, was used by Columbus because he was under the impression that these islands provided a new route to the *Indies,* a term that at that time included the whole of eastern Asia, whose wealth had been described by Marco Polo a century earlier.

A wide range of environmental factors has influenced architecture in the Caribbean Islands, and these factors differ from island to island, as well as on in-dividual islands. There is to be found within this area the complete range of phys-ical land characteristics—mountains, volcanoes, flatlands, forests, deserts, and so forth. Each of these situations affected building material availability, and each presented unique demands for shelter and comfort requirements.

The Caribbean Sea lies south of the Tropic of Cancer and north of ten de-grees north latitude; although the area is all considered to be *tropical,* there is con-siderable variation in climate characteristics. Some areas are arid, almost without

Fig. 1. Map of the Caribbean Sea

Fig. 2. The mountains of Haiti, demonstrating one of the many moods of Hispaniola

rainfall, while others receive excessive moisture. All of the Caribbean islands, however, experience almost daily clear skies and sunshine, with year-round temperatures ranging between 75 and 85 degrees F. Trade winds from the northeast serve as a welcome cooling factor, but most of the islands are also subject to occasional hurricane devastation.

The Amerindians who occupied the Caribbean islands before the arrival of Europeans responded to these geographic and climatic factors in their simplistic

Fig. 3. The coast of Sint Maarten, a typical tropical Caribbean shore scene

Fig. 4. Typical indigenous Caribbean construction

architecture. Similarly, the earliest European settlers of necessity resorted to basic approaches for shelter. As soon as possible, though, the settlers yielded to the nostalgia of building designs recalled from the mother country. Professional architectural assistance was usually not available, however, and the recollection of *correct* architectural styles and details was often inaccurate. Builders' handbooks were helpful but frequently required a translation from traditional European building materials to those that were available locally. There was also usually a lag in style,

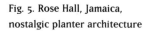
Fig. 5. Rose Hall, Jamaica,
nostalgic planter architecture

so that architectural changes occurring in Europe might not be reflected in colonial examples until thirty years or more later.

The most significant aspect of this stage of architectural development in the Caribbean was that the closer the architecture came to that of the mother country, the less appropriate it usually was to the tropics. Although familiar building techniques used by local artisans eventually did help to achieve the transition to a more appropriate Caribbean architecture in some instances, many building types never made the shift.

The actual and imagined benefits from control of the Caribbean islands produced such an intense rivalry among European nations that sometimes the Caribbean colonies exercised more clout in the mother countries than did the North American colonies. The North American colonists' complaint of "taxation without representation" was not heard in the British West Indies, where Caribbean planters frequently became influential members of the British Parliament.

The Europeans primarily involved in the competition for Caribbean control were the Spanish, French, English, Dutch, and Danes, and each contributed, in varying degrees, to the architectural development of the islands. Historical control of an island sometimes changed with considerable frequency, so there is seldom influence from a single country but rather from multiple European architectural influences. Furthermore, much of the delight of Caribbean architecture would have been absent without the contributions of African slaves and the various Asian indentured laborers and their descendants.

No architecture developed that could be defined as *Caribbean* and that would apply to the entire area. Because of the independent nature of each island, distinctions between their architectures persisted, even between those of islands colonized by the same European country.

Climate undoubtedly led to some degree of architectural uniformity, once it was realized that the basic function of a tropical building was to offer simple protection from rain and sun. This awareness eliminated many of the superficial elements of nostalgic colonial building. More appreciation for the out-of-doors allowed the garden to become an important part of the living environment, which led to connecting architectural elements between the out-of-doors and the building enclosure: galleries, verandas, porches, balconies, larger windows, louvered shutters, walls composed almost entirely of doors, and so on. Even the extensive use of fretwork, although undeniably decorative, had climatic advantages, for it offered a degree of privacy while still filtering the bright sunlight, allowing air to flow into the building and maintaining a visual connection with the outdoors.

Wood was the predominant building material in the early colonial Caribbean. Brick and tile were available for more formal buildings because they were popular ballast materials on sailing ships coming from Europe. Eventually, some brick was manufactured in the Caribbean, but its popularity declined when its poor resistance to earthquakes became apparent.

When paint became readily available in the area, color replaced the previous natural hues of Caribbean buildings. Paint offered fascinating new ways of expressing the exuberance and gaiety of African traditions, but it, too, was used differently on different islands.

Thus the architectural expressions of the Caribbean islands are as varied as the islands themselves, and yet a general harmonious unity exists within this variety because of the many common parameters that shaped the architecture.

CHAPTER 1

THE EARLY CARIBBEAN

THE PRE-COLUMBIAN CARIBBEAN

We assume that there were inhabitants of the Caribbean area several millennia before the first European explorers came to this part of the world and that these earliest settlers probably came from Asia via a land connection between Asia and Alaska, where the Bering Strait is now. They gradually scattered over North and South America and then to the Caribbean, coalescing into separate groups with distinct cultures. It is known that, about 3500 B.C., a Stone Age people called Siboney (or Ciboney) migrated from Florida to the West Indies.

Extensive remains of Amerindian civilizations exist in many locations. However, few specifics are known about them because of the absence of writing systems. Most of what has been learned has been from examining artifacts found during archaeological excavations.

EARLY SPANISH EXPLORATION

Christopher Columbus made four voyages to the West Indies, and we find considerable controversy over the exact routes taken on these trips. On the first, in 1492–93, evidence indicates that he visited the Bahamas, Cuba, and Hispaniola (now Haiti and the Dominican Republic).

On his second voyage, 1493–96, accompanied by his brother Diego, he made initial visits to Dominica, Marie Galante, Guadeloupe, Montserrat, Antigua, St. Martin, the Virgin Islands, Puerto Rico, and Jamaica. He sighted St. Kitts but did not land on this island. Before leaving the area, he also revisited Hispaniola and Cuba.

The third voyage, 1498–1500, took Columbus to Trinidad and the coast of South America, which he assumed to be Asia. He sighted Grenada, then returned to Spain by way of Hispaniola and Puerto Rico.

On his fourth voyage, 1502–4, Columbus was accompanied by his son Ferdinand. St. Lucians claim that theirs is the island that Columbus did *not* discover; others maintain that he visited St. Lucia in 1502, the year that he went ashore in Martinique. It is known that, on this last voyage, he sailed west along the coasts of Puerto Rico, Hispaniola, and Jamaica before going south to the coasts of Central and South America. He then turned north and again sailed past the Greater Antilles to return home.

With these four voyages, Columbus visited or sighted almost all of the major Caribbean islands. Spain thus laid claim to the entire Caribbean area, referring

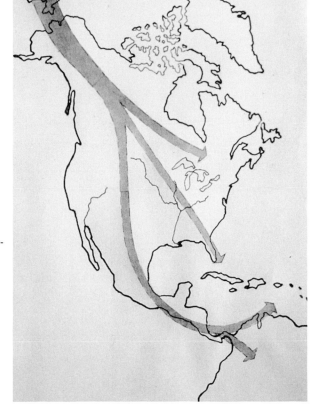

Fig. 6. Probable route of the earliest Caribbean inhabitants

Fig. 7. First voyage of Columbus

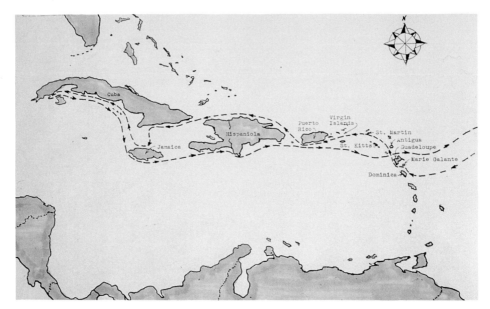

Fig. 8. Second voyage of Columbus

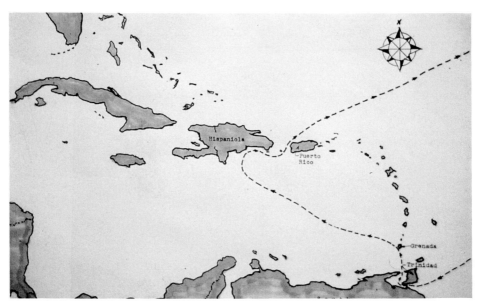

Fig. 9. Third voyage of Columbus

to it as the "Spanish Lake." Gold was the primary goal of the Spaniards, however, and they quickly lost interest in the Lesser Antilles when they did not find this precious metal there.

THE CARIBBEAN AMERINDIANS

The Amerindians first encountered by Columbus were the Arawaks, who came from South America. In the mid-eighth century A.D., they began moving into

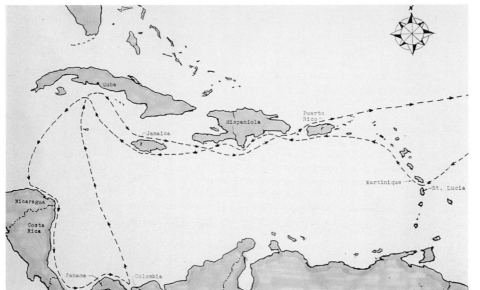

Fig. 10. Fourth voyage of Columbus

Fig. 11. Early print of Arawak Indians

the West Indies and by 1500 had spread throughout all the islands. They formed a number of groups, including the Lucayo in the Bahamas, the Taíno in the Greater Antilles, and the Igneri in the Lesser Antilles. These were peace-loving people who gradually blended with the Siboney population. They farmed, fished, and hunted small mammals and birds for survival. When Columbus made his first voyage, the Arawaks told him that they had suffered from raids by canni-bals who lived in the Lesser Antilles to the southeast. These were the Caribs, a warlike tribe who had also originated on the South American mainland and who had driven most of the Arawaks out of the Lesser Antilles shortly before the arrival of the Spaniards.

All of the Amerindians in the Caribbean region suffered badly at the hands of the European settlers. They were enslaved, and many died as the result of harsh treatment. Others committed suicide. Many more succumbed to European diseases to which they had no immunity. By 1700, the Caribbean had ceased to be an Amerindian region. Today, in all of the Caribbean islands only a few hundred Caribs survive; they live on the island of Dominica on a reserve established by the British government in 1903.

Because the Caribbean Amerindians had no writing, they left no descriptions of their architecture. In his journals, Columbus described an Arawak settlement as a collection of loosely arranged dwellings, without streets. He saw tentlike huts made of palm fronds.

Because the Arawaks were seagoing and lived to a great extent on seafoods, most of their villages were close to the coast or near rivers. Settlements ranged

Fig. 12. Reconstructed Amerindian hut, Nassau, Bahamas

from single units of families to towns of fifty or more houses, which were sometimes arranged around ball courts.

One of the largest discovered Arawak sites in the Caribbean was White Marl, east of Spanish Town, Jamaica, where considerable excavation has been done. The village commanded an extensive view from the top of a hill at whose base flowed the Rio Cobre, which emptied into the Caribbean. (A storm in 1722 changed the course of Rio Cobre, and it no longer flows along the foot of White Marl Hill.) Excavations at this site in 1969 revealed nine postholes placed in a circle approximately fourteen feet in diameter, with a center post. It is assumed that lengths of wild cane, rush, bamboo, or palm were fixed between the exterior posts, secured to them with small branches or vines. A cone-shaped roof was framed to the center post and thatched with grass and palm fronds. This configuration is similar to residential structures excavated in other locations in the Caribbean. Good conjectural reconstructions may be seen at the Tibes Ceremonial Center near Ponce, Puerto Rico; in the Antigua Museum in St. John's; and on the grounds of the Department of Archives in Nassau, Bahamas. In the Nassau example, there is the typical center pole plus twelve poles in a circle, each seven feet five inches from the center.

We find, in addition to circular plans, hexagons and rectangles. Another variation was a primitive arrangement in which the roof structure emerged directly from the ground in a tentlike shape. These various shelters, called *carbets* and *ajoupas* and *canayes,* were simple in construction yet could stand up to strong winds, even hurricanes. We assume that cooking occurred outdoors. The house of the chief, whether round or rectangular, was typically larger than the other residences.

Carib houses were similar in plan to those of the Arawaks, although sometimes oval in plan. The houses were grouped around a central plaza in which a fireplace was located. In both Arawak and Carib houses, furnishings were restricted to wooden stools and tables and hammocks, the last an Amerindian invention.

CHAPTER 2

HISTORICAL BACKGROUND AND URBANIZATION

THE ENGLISH ISLANDS

Much British colonization and development occurred under the financing and administration of private enterprise, organized into joint-stock companies. Under such a development, patterns of urbanization were not always shaped by the dictates of the motherland but nevertheless showed strong influences from England. Larger towns typically had the formality of contemporary European baroque cities, with central spaces that may have recalled Picadilly Circus or Trafalgar Square. In the smaller Caribbean towns, the village green concept often accommodated the courthouse and the parish church.

Jamaica

When Columbus visited Jamaica in 1494 on his second voyage, he named it St. Jago. The Spanish occupied the island in 1509 and, in the following year, founded the first capital, Sevilla la Nueva, on the north coast near an ancient Arawak village. Because of its unhealthy position close to swamps the town was

Fig. 13. Caribbean map locating Jamaica

abandoned fourteen years later, and the seat of the government was moved across the island to St. Jago de la Vega.

In 1655, the English failed in an attempt to take the island of Hispaniola from the Spanish. Rather than return to England in shame, the force sailed west and took Jamaica, which was weakly held by the Spanish. It was the first island taken forcibly by the British from the Spanish. The name of the capital, St. Jago de la Vega, was changed to Spanish Town. Although no Spanish buildings survive, the layout of the town nucleus remains, with later British civic buildings benefiting from the unity of the original layout.

As had been the practice in medieval England, British Jamaica was divided into parishes. Although in England each parish had a governing body and a church, in Jamaica parishes eventually served merely as convenient divisions for controlling large land tracts.

In 1692 the town of Port Royal was destroyed by earthquake. In search of a new place to live, the survivors decided on the lower part of the Liguanea Plain of St. Andrew Parish and plans were drawn for the new town of Kingston. Its physical layout had a formal quality. The major north-south artery was King Street, the major east-west artery Queen Street. At what would have been the intersection of these two streets was placed a central square resembling the London residential squares popular at that time. The parish church was located on the south side of the square. Space was allocated for a Governor's House, although there is no evidence that one ever materialized. By 1702, however, the lots around the square had all been acquired by the most influential citizens.

The square was eventually taken over by the army, as indicated by the designation Place d'Arme on a 1764 map. This change is not surprising, for there was considerable military activity in the Caribbean in the eighteenth century. Army barracks and magazines were constructed around the square, and troops drilled

Fig. 14. Old print of Spanish Town, Jamaica, on Emancipation Day, 1838

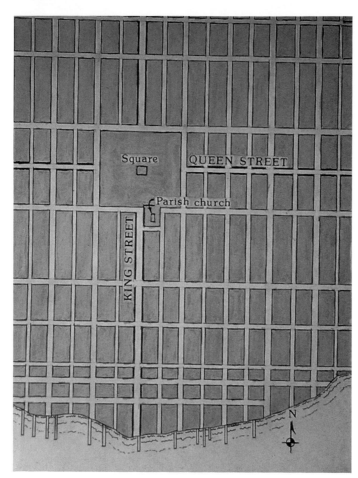

Fig. 15. Plan of Kingston, Jamaica

Fig. 16. Old print, ca. 1860, view of King Street, Kingston, Jamaica

Fig. 17. Mandeville, Jamaica, laid out like an English village

in the open area, giving it the name Parade, which persists to this day. The barracks were moved about 1790, and the area eventually became a park, opened to the public in 1872, the year that Kingston became the capital of Jamaica.

Despite the importance of the square to early Kingston, the nerve center of the city was Harbour Street, where the major wharves and shipping facilities of the island were located. At that time, the shoreline was defined by the south edge of Harbour Street, until filling moved the shoreline south and Port Royal Street was created.

Mid-nineteenth-century Kingston had a downtown area where colonnaded business places stood at street level, with wood-frame residential units above. The streets were unpaved. Disastrous fires destroyed large sections of Kingston in 1780, in 1843, in 1862, and again in 1882. The most devastating event, however, was the 1907 earthquake and the accompanying fires. Most of the buildings in Kingston were destroyed or badly damaged, and an estimated 1,500 people were killed.

Several small towns in Jamaica show the heritage of the English village. One is Mandeville, in Manchester Parish, which began as a small early-nineteenth-century town. The relatively cool climate resulting from its 2,000-foot elevation made the town a favorite for English residents. The courthouse and the parish church were important planned ingredients in this English village green concept.

St. Kitts (St. Christopher)

We do not know whether Columbus named this island after himself or after his patron saint, St. Christopher. Mt. Liamuiga, prominent on the island, was once an active volcano, and the volcanic origin of the island is apparent in the black sand beaches and the sulphur fumes still evident around Brimstone Hill.

Fig. 18. Caribbean map locating St. Kitts

Fig. 19. Plan of Basseterre, St. Kitts.

British settlers were taken to St. Kitts in 1624 by Sir Thomas Warner, making it the first English colony in the Caribbean. Both Britain and France exercised sovereignty over parts of the island until 1713 when, by the Treaty of Utrecht, the French were required to leave.

The streets of Basseterre, the capital and principal seaport, are laid out in a random pattern. The capital's center is the Circus, built in the tradition of Picadilly Circus in London. Defined by a variety of buildings, it is a hive of pedestrians and vehicles. The Berkeley Memorial Drinking Fountain and Clock stands at its center.

Fig. 20. The Circus, major center of Basseterre, St. Kitts, today

Fig. 21. Independence Square, pivotal center of Basseterre, St. Kitts, in the eighteenth century

In the second half of the eighteenth century, the pivot of political, commercial, and social life in Basseterre was Pall Mall Square, now called Independence Square. It was also the site of the slave market. The Roman Catholic Co-cathedral, the Courthouse, and numerous residences faced onto the square. When the Courthouse was destroyed by fire in 1982, its replacement was built on another site, taking with it much of the locale's civic activity and leaving behind a primarily residential square.

Another significant open area is Warner Park where, in 1983, the newly designed flag of St. Kitts/Nevis was first raised, signifying independence from Britain.

Antigua

Columbus visited Antigua in 1493 and named the island after a church in Seville, Santa Maria la Antigua, in which he had asked the blessing of St. Christopher before starting on his second voyage. In 1632, the English moved settlers to Antigua from St. Kitts and Nevis; with the exception of a brief occupation by the French in 1666, it has remained British ever since.

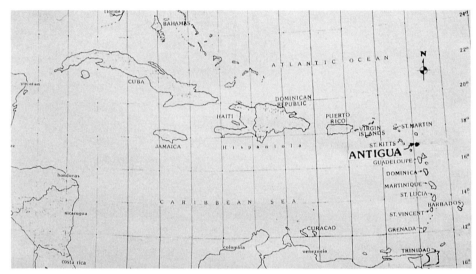

Fig. 22. Caribbean map locating Antigua

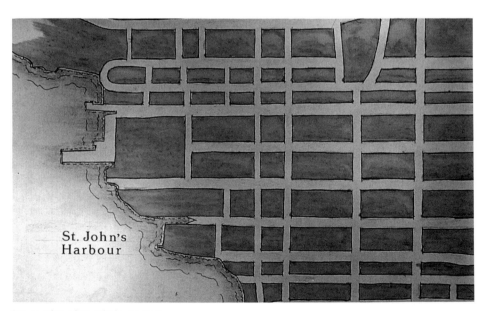

Fig. 23. Plan of St. John's, Antigua

The capital of Antigua is St. John's, located on an excellent deep-water harbor and one of the first towns in the Caribbean planned with broad parallel avenues and narrower cross-streets. Redcliffe Quay, which was a slave-holding area near the waterfront, has been transformed into a series of shops. The most prominent building in St. John's is its Anglican cathedral, located on a prominent hilltop.

St. Lucia

St. Lucia, one of the larger of the Windward Islands, was settled by the English in 1639 but in 1640 the colony was wiped out by the native Caribs. Subsequently, St. Lucia changed hands between the English and the French thirteen times, until it finally became English in 1803, the last of the Antilles to fall from French into English hands. In the development of the island, French influence has been strong, and most of the inhabitants have been Roman Catholic. St. Lucia is of particular interest to Jamaicans because it was from the naval headquarters at Pigeon Island, off St. Lucia, that Admiral George Rodney set sail to defeat the French fleet in the Battle of the Saints, when the French were on their way to invade Jamaica.

Castries, the capital, has a fine landlocked harbor and was at one time the principal coaling station for the British West Indies. Castries has burned to the ground five times. In the disastrous fire of 1948, the Roman Catholic cathedral was the only large building to survive. Columbus Square is the center of the town, and the reconstructed buildings that surround it reflect some apparent French influence.

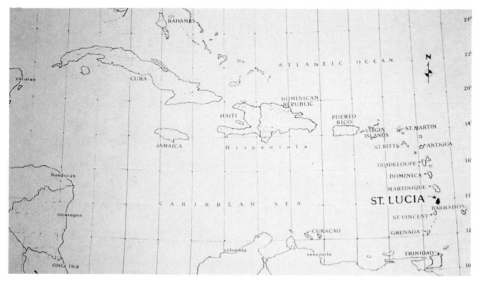

Fig. 24. Caribbean map locating St. Lucia

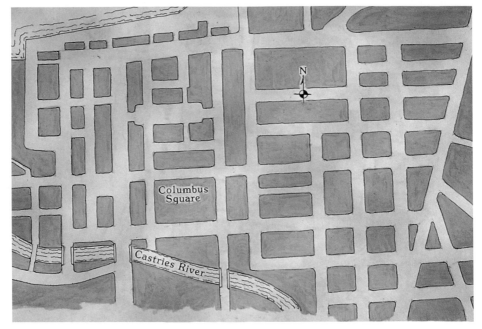

Fig. 25. Plan of Castries, St. Lucia

Fig. 26. Columbus Square, Castries, St. Lucia

Barbados

Barbados is the most easterly of the West Indian islands, too far off the beaten path to be bothered by would-be possessors. The first Europeans to visit Barbados were the Portuguese, sometime in the early sixteenth century. They named the island Los Barbados (the Bearded), for the beardlike tendrils hanging from the wild fig trees. The Portuguese did not settle here, however, and the island re-

Fig. 27. Caribbean map locating Barbados

Fig. 28. Plan of Bridgetown, Barbados

mained without nationality until 1605, when the crew of an English ship claimed it for their king. After landing in 1625, Englishman John Powell returned in 1627 with eighty colonists. Since then it has been uninterruptedly British and is still frequently referred to as "Little England." By 1640, Barbados had a population of about 18,000, which equaled that of the larger mainland English colonies such as Virginia and New England. Coral limestone covers the greater part of the island and provides a valued building material.

Bridgetown, the capital of Barbados, has a waterfront that has been important throughout its history. In addition to shipping activity, ships were brought here for overhauling, cleaning, and caulking. The town seems to have been allowed to grow in an irregular and haphazard manner. Many of its streets are narrow and accommodate both pedestrians and vehicles with difficulty. Barbadians are proud of Bridgetown's Trafalgar Square and its statue of Lord Nelson, which was erected before its London counterpart.

Grenada

Grenada, the southernmost of the Windward Islands, was named Concepción by Columbus. Fierce Caribs were able to hold the island for 150 years after that first sighting, however, and no Spanish ever settled here. It was colonized by the French in 1650, ceded to the British in 1763, and held again by the French from 1779 to 1783 when, as a result of Admiral George Rodney's memorable triumph, the British won it for good.

St. George's, the capital, is built on a mile-long peninsula that forms one side of a fine almost-landlocked inner harbor, the Carenage. This harbor is actually a volcanic crater, with St. George's built on its rim. Here sailing vessels could be turned on their sides for caulking and repair.

The irregular coastline and hilly terrain contribute to a chaotic street pattern. The town was first laid out in 1705 by M. de Bellair, the French governor, and planning was continued by the English when they took possession. A ridge divides St. George's into two towns. To get from one to the other, one must climb the ridge or go through Sendall Tunnel, a ten-foot-wide passage dug in 1894.

Buildings that line the waterfront, as well as those perched on the hills around the Carenage, show considerable influence from the days when the island was a French possession. The brick and the red clay tiles used in construction came to Grenada on the ships that sailed here to fill up with spices and sugar. The older buildings also frequently have wrought-iron balconies that are French in style.

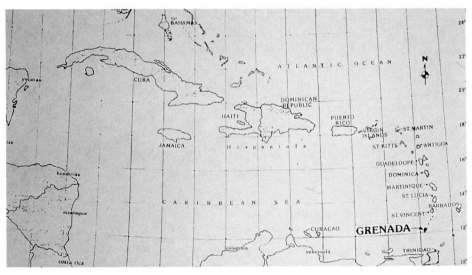

Fig. 29. Caribbean map locating Grenada

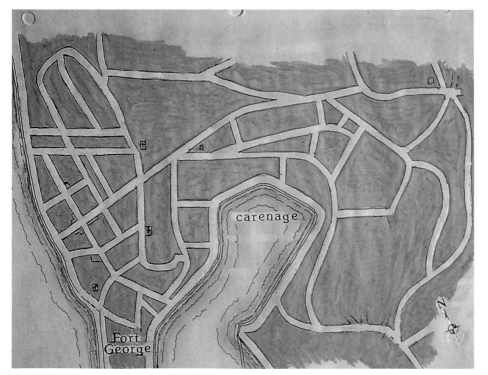

Fig. 30. Plan of St. George's, Grenada

Fig. 31. Sendall Tunnel, connecting two
sections of St. George's, Grenada

Trinidad

Trinidad is the southernmost and largest of the Lesser Antilles. Columbus claimed it for Spain and named it La Trinidad for a group of three low hills on the southeast corner of the island, off which he first anchored. The desirability of attracting workers to the island prompted the Spanish to introduce the *Cedula de Población,* a policy that granted land to non-Spanish settlers. It attracted many new settlers, particularly from the French islands. These were joined by thousands of French royalists from Martinique and other French Caribbean islands, who took up residence in Trinidad during the French Revolution. During its Spanish tenure, the island was subject to raids by the Dutch and the French. In

Fig. 32. Caribbean map locating Trinidad

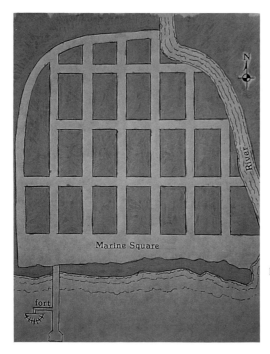

Fig. 33. 1757 layout of Port of Spain, Trinidad

1797, British forces overcame the Spanish, resulting in the Treaty of Amiens in 1802, when Trinidad was ceded to Britain.

Port of Spain, the capital of Trinidad/Tobago, has always been a busy waterfront and commercial center. The original Spanish town was laid out on a rigid grid, although European design forms were not strictly imposed by either the Spanish occupiers or the immigrant French. Even though the Spanish occupied Trinidad two centuries longer than they occupied any other of the Lesser Antilles, they left almost no cultural mark on the island, and the great fire of 1808 destroyed most architectural symbols of Spanish occupation in the capital. The original city of Port of Spain was bounded on the south by the Caribbean Sea

Fig. 34. Old print of 1851 waterfront, Port of Spain, Trinidad

Fig. 35. Woodford Square, downtown Port of Spain, Trinidad

Fig. 36. Victoria Square, residential park, Port of Spain, Trinidad

and on the east by the Ariapita River. The last Spanish governor, Don José María Chacón, deflected the river from its original position, leaving a dry gully.

A print of King's Wharf and South Cay in 1851 shows a landmark that is still prominent on the waterfront of Port of Spain. Built on filled land, the octagonal white lighthouse leans a bit and is nonoperational, but it stands as a pleasant reminder of days past (see plate 1). The city has a number of attractive landscaped urban spaces. Marine Square, a plaza near the water, dates from Spanish days and was at one time bordered by handsome houses. It is now an active commercial area, since 1962 known as Independence Square. Woodford Square, formerly Brunswick Square, central to downtown Port of Spain, provides a landscaped setting onto which a number of significant buildings face.

Several small parks grace more recently established neighborhoods, as well as the 200-acre Queen's Park Savannah, claimed to be the first designated recreation ground in the West Indies.

Bahamas

In 1492, Columbus first landed in the New World at Guanahani, the Lucayan (Arawak) name for the Bahamian island that Columbus renamed San Salvador. England laid formal claim to the Bahamas in 1629, but the islands remained virtually untouched until English settlers arrived on Eleuthera in 1648. By 1670, the island of New Providence had 300 inhabitants, and in 1690 a listing of buildings in Charles Towne (now Nassau) included the original Christ Church Cathedral, Fort Nassau, and 160 houses.

Although the Bahamas were attacked by both France and Spain during the eighteenth century, outside of a brief occupation by a small U.S. naval force in

Fig. 37. West Indies map locating the Bahamas

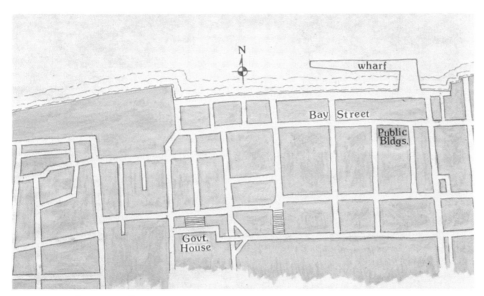

Fig. 38. Plan of Nassau, Bahamas

1776 and some later unsuccessful attacks by the Spanish, the islands have remained peacefully British. In 1783, many Loyalists fled with their slaves from the
newly independent United States to the Bahamas.

In 1729, Charles Towne was renamed Nassau for King William III of the
House of Orange–Nassau. The line of the original waterfront was then at Bay
Street, with the streets running more or less parallel and perpendicular to it. At
first the Public Buildings directly overlooked the water, but land filling to the
north created space for Rawson Square in front of the Public Buildings.

Mount Fitzwilliam, running east-west through Nassau, is responsible for several interesting urban features in the town. A cut through the hill allows Market
Street to maintain a gradual slope as it enters Grant's Town and becomes Main

Fig. 39. Gregory Arch, Nassau, Bahamas

Fig. 40. Pedestrian steps, end of Frederick Street, Nassau, Bahamas

Street. Gregory Arch, which provides a bridge over this depression for direct access to the east gate of the Government House grounds, was built in 1852 by the surveyor general, J. J. Burnside, and named after John Gregory, governor at that time. In 1854, iron railings imported from England were added to the bridge.

Fig. 41. Queen's Staircase,
access to Fort Fincastle,
Nassau, Bahamas

The southern end of vehicular Frederick Street is at Prince's Street. At that point, because of the steepness of the terrain, handsome pedestrian steps climb south to East Hill Street.

Farther east in town, at the south end of Elizabeth Street, lies the quarry in Bennet's Hill that provided the limestone for many of Nassau's early buildings. The Queen's Staircase located here provided access from the level of Elizabeth Street through the quarry up to Fort Fincastle. Supposedly cut out of solid rock around 1793 by slaves, the steps were later named in honor of Queen Victoria.

THE SPANISH ISLANDS

Towns in Spanish colonies were laid out in accordance with strict requirements set down by the mother country. Following the dictates of Catholic priests and the Law of the Indies, streets were arranged at right angles to one another, plazas created, and sites determined for major buildings. The discipline of this spatial pattern was faithfully adhered to from the sixteenth to the nineteenth centuries.

Puerto Rico

Puerto Rico is the easternmost and smallest of the Greater Antilles, named by Columbus San Juan Bautista. When Ponce de León arrived in 1508 to be its first governor, he is said to have exclaimed, "Que puerto rico!" (What a rich port!) and so named his settlement. There were about 30,000 Arawaks occupying the island at that time, but by 1580 they had practically disappeared.

The first Spanish settlement in Puerto Rico was at Caparra, a low-lying settle-

Fig. 42. Caribbean map locating Puerto Rico

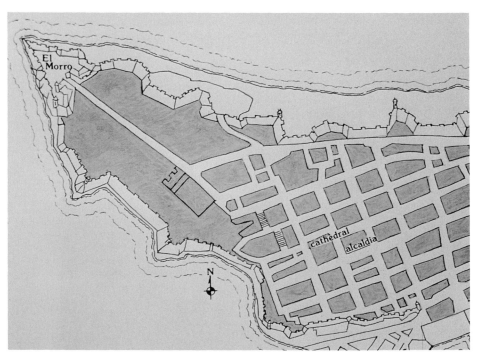

Fig. 43. Plan of Old San Juan, Puerto Rico

ment plagued with mosquitoes. In 1519, royal authorization was given to move the settlement to the breezy islet now called San Juan Island, a move that was accomplished in 1521. Also in that year, a name switch made Puerto Rico the island name and San Juan the town. This town became the second-oldest European settlement in the New World, after Santo Domingo. The layout of Old San Juan is basically a grid, concentrated within an area that covers less than half a square mile. The colonial streets are narrow and in the late nineteenth century were paved with blue-glazed bricks, *adoquines,* which were cast using slag from European iron foundries.

Because of the hilly nature of Old San Juan, several of the original streets became, of necessity, pedestrian step streets. Two remain: Callejón de las Monjas and Caleta del Hospital. The sloping Plaza of the Cathedral onto which San Juan Cathedral faces is the oldest of several plazas. On Plaza de Armas, the main sixteenth-century square, the city's early inhabitants drilled in preparation for attacks. In time, this plaza became an important governmental as well as social center. The four 100-year-old statues that currently preside over it represent the four seasons.

Construction on the wall surrounding colonial San Juan began in the 1630s and was not completed until the late 1700s (see plate 2). It was patrolled day and night, with six gates that were closed at sundown to cut off access to the city. San Juan Gate, built in 1639, is the only one surviving. The San Juan wall is the only one built by Spain in the New World that remains basically intact.

Other towns and villages in Puerto Rico follow the typical Spanish plan, built around a central plaza with its church, with streets laid out in a grid. Ponce, founded in 1692 on Puerto Rico's south coast, boasts Plaza las Delicias, a

Fig. 44. Caleta del Hospital, pedestrian step street, San Juan, Puerto Rico

Fig. 45. San Juan Gate, 1639, Puerto Rico

delightful town center where are located the cathedral, city hall, historic fire station, and other significant buildings. Fountains, trees, and benches add to its charm. Ponce was known as "the Pearl of the South" for its elegant houses and wide, tree-shaded streets. An ambitious renovation of a sixty-six-block downtown area is currently under way, and many historic buildings have been accurately restored.

Cuba

Cuba is the largest of the Caribbean islands. Its early inhabitants are supposed to have been the Siboneys from Florida. At a later date, about A.D. 1100, the Taíno (Arawaks) migrated here from Hispaniola. The island derived its name from the native Cubanacan, referring to a legendary Indian maiden. The name Juana was used by the Spaniards, after the son of Ferdinand and Isabella. This gave way to Ferdinandina, then to Santiago, then Ave Maria, before the return to the original Amerindian name.

Although the first settlers arrived in 1511, they lost interest when the small amount of available gold had been taken from the mines. However, fortifications were erected after the 1555 sack of Havana by the French. The old city wall was begun in 1663, completed in 1740, and subsequently revised by the various colonial governments. It eventually became an impediment to the city's growth.

In 1762, the British occupied the island until the Treaty of Paris gave Havana back to Spain in exchange for Florida the following year. Internal unrest in Cuba and frustrated attempts at revolution, plus the sinking of the *Maine* in Havana Harbor, led to the Spanish-American War, which culminated in an 1898 peace treaty in which Spain relinquished claims to Cuba.

Fig. 46. Caribbean map locating Cuba

Fig. 47. Plan of Old Havana, Cuba

Because of its fine harbor, Havana had quickly become Spain's navigation center in the Americas and replaced Santo Domingo as the most important Spanish colonial city. Its original center was Church Square, located near the port, where the first parish church was built. Known as Arms Square (Plaza de las Armas) after the troops from Real Fuerza Castle began to drill here, it remains an impressive urban space with a shady park surrounded by significant buildings. The only remaining wooden pavement in Havana is on the west side of the plaza; its original function was to muffle the sounds of military traffic.

Old Square (Plaza Vieja) became the focal point of Havana's commercial and social life after Arms Square was taken over by the military (see plate 3). Surrounded by arcaded buildings, Old Square became the city's primary market center. A modern underground parking garage that has raised the surface of the square provides an unfortunate interruption to the original spatial quality. Cathedral Square (Plaza de la Catedral) is considered Havana's most architecturally harmonious square. In addition to the baroque cathedral, magnificent mansions that provided the spatial definition for the square have been restored and adapted as a gallery, restaurants, museums, and so on. Old Havana also has two smaller but significant squares: Christ Square and San Francisco Square. The Old City, despite its deterioration, has remained essentially unchanged for centuries and in 1982 was classified as a world heritage site by UNESCO.

During the 1925–33 administration of Gerardo Machado, the French architect Le Forestier was commissioned to do a reordering and beautification of Havana and U.S. architects John M. Carrère and Thomas Hastings, as well as Ralph Adams Cram and Bertram Grosvenor Goodhue, were involved in significant architectural work.

Fig. 48. Arms Square, Havana, Cuba

Fig. 49. Tree-lined Prado, Havana, Cuba

Although this urban study deals primarily with Old Havana, Paseo de Martí (Prado) lies just west of the old city, a handsome, tree-lined promenade whose generously wide walk has large geometric terrazzo patterns. Stone benches divide its outer edges from the streets. The buildings that line the streets, despite their architectural variety, are unified by the continuous arcades at street level, under all the buildings. Prado originates at the north waterfront near Punta Fortress and is a major thoroughfare until it encounters Máximo Gómez (Monte).

Smaller Cuban towns demonstrate the usual Spanish plan, with the church in a prominent location and public buildings surrounding a central square.

Dominican Republic

Columbus called the island of Hispaniola La Isla Española because he thought it resembled Spain. The Amerindians there were Arawaks and Caribs, the latter having wrested most of the island from the former. The native Indian population disappeared rapidly, either killed in battle or by disease. After Spain acquired Mexico and Peru, Española (eventually corrupted to Hispaniola) was viewed with less importance. In 1697, by the Treaty of Ryswick, Spain was forced to recognize the dominion of France over the western third of the island. In 1822, the whole island was subdued by residents of the French portion, who remained in control for twenty-two years. In 1865, the country was reannexed to Spain and then once again was prey to revolutionaries and assassinations. A U.S. military government ruled the country from 1916 until 1924, when constitutional government was restored.

When on his second voyage Columbus found no trace of the settlement that

Fig. 50. Caribbean map locating Dominican Republic

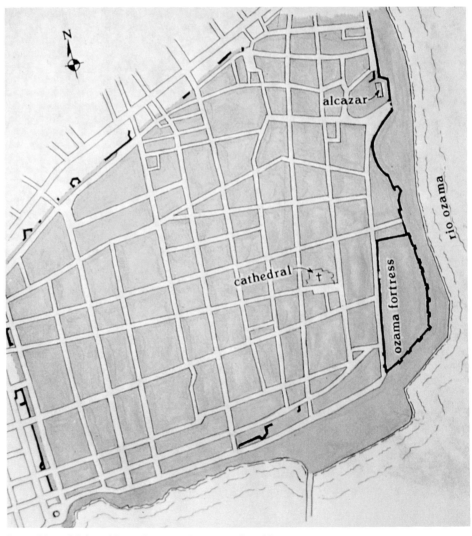

Fig. 51. Plan of Colonial Santo Domingo, Dominican Republic

he had established on his first, he founded a new city farther east on the north coast of what is now the Dominican Republic, naming it La Isabella, after the queen. In 1498, however, gold was discovered on the south coast, and the occupants of La Isabella moved there and named their new settlement Santo Domingo de Guzmán. This became the capital not only of this island but of all the lands claimed by Spain at that time.

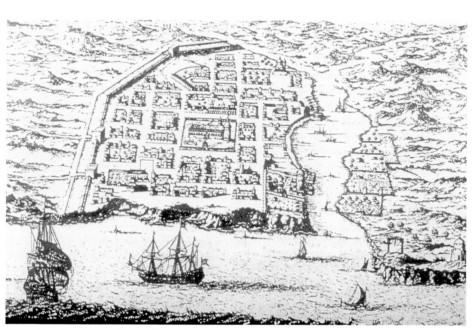

Fig. 52. Plan drawing ca. 1690 of Santo Domingo, Dominican Republic

Fig. 53. El Conde Gate, Santo Domingo, Dominican Republic

Colonial Santo Domingo basically followed a gridiron plan, enclosed by a wall, remnants of which still exist to define the area. Of the four gates to the city, three still exist. Diego's Gate, built in 1509, is on the river side of the city near the home of Diego Columbus, son of Christopher and the second governor of the island. Misercordia Gate or the Old Savanna Gate, also built in the sixteenth century, was named for the small chapel nearby. El Conde Street, which runs the entire east-west dimension of the colonial city, terminates at El Conde Gate on the western edge. The inscription above this eighteenth-century gate reads "Dulce et decorum pro Patria Mori" (It is sweet and decorous to die for one's country.)

Colonial Santo Domingo has a number of pleasant plazas on which prominent buildings are located and in which are placed monuments to the country's heroes.

THE FRENCH ISLANDS

The French Islands experienced a variety of disruptions in addition to the frequent change of ownership characteristic of all Caribbean islands. Earthquakes, volcanic eruptions, and revolutions in various locations undoubtedly kept cities on these islands from developing in similar ways. Nor was the French West India Company able to exert much influence, as it existed for only ten years. Whatever the reasons, French influence is much more apparent in colonial building than in planning.

Haiti

When Columbus first visited Hispaniola, the island was called Hayti, which meant "mountainous" in the Arawak language. As with the Dominican Republic, the 1697 Treaty of Ryswick ceded the western third of Hispaniola to France; the French named this section St. Domingue.

Fig. 54. Caribbean map locating Haiti

Fig. 55. Plan of Cap
Haïtien, Haiti

The outbreak of the French Revolution in 1789 awakened the desire for freedom in the various French colonies, leading to slave uprisings. In 1793, a French decree abolished slavery in St. Domingue, but the decree was rescinded and a rebellion followed. The leader of this rebellion was Toussaint L'Ouverture, who was captured and sent to France, where he died. Two new leaders, however, kept the fires of rebellion blazing. Jean-Jacques Dessalines and Alexandre Pétion led the rebels to victory, and in 1804 the former French colony became a free and independent nation, and the name Haiti was substituted for the French St. Domingue. After Dessaline's death in 1806, Henri Christophe ruled the land until his death in 1820.

Cap Haïtien, on the north coast, was founded by the Spanish in 1667, using the Spanish colonial city model. The French renamed it Le Cap Français, and for the last half of the eighteenth century it was considered the Paris of the entire island. After its destruction in 1802 during the revolution, it was eventually rebuilt by Christophe and renamed Cap Haïtien. The earthquake of 1842 destroyed many of its buildings of architectural value.

Port-au-Prince, founded in 1749, became the capital of Haiti. Its plan is basically a grid, with a number of irregular, randomly located streets. An interesting departure from the grid occurs in the Champ de Mars, with its Versailles-like diagonal treatment of the streets. This area, onto which the National Palace faces,

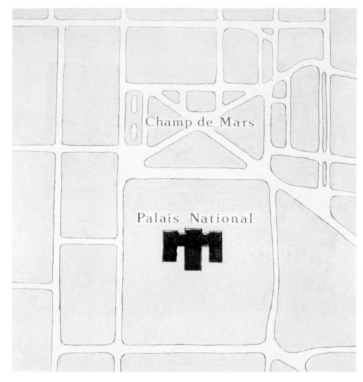

Fig. 56. Plan of Champ
de Mars, Port-au-
Prince, Haiti

was laid out in 1953. In the newer parts of the town, broad boulevards contrast with the narrow streets of the old section.

It would be negligent in discussing the urban scene in Haiti not to mention the "tap-taps," those marvelously decorative open-air minibuses without which the streets of Port-au-Prince would seem drab (see plate 4). They symbolize the energy of the city, each a unique sideshow that combine to create a delightful circus.

An open market off Avenue John Brown Lalue in Port-au-Prince, Haiti, requires no architecture to demonstrate the kinetic energy that characterizes the Caribbean market (see plate 5).

Martinique

The name Martinique is derived from the Carib Madinina, meaning "Island of Flowers." The island was not colonized until 1635, when a Norman nobleman landed with a group of French settlers and built Fort St. Pierre. The island experienced attacks by the Dutch and the British, the latter gaining possession in 1794–1802 and in 1809–14, after which it became and remained French. For a time, Martinique was the most prosperous of the French colonies, producing sugar, coffee, cocoa, and indigo.

Before 1902, the most important town in Martinique was St. Pierre, the capital and busiest port. The center of the island's intellectual life, it was known as the Paris of the West Indies. In 1902 Mont Pelée erupted, destroying St. Pierre and its 30,000 inhabitants. Existing ruins attest to the force of this disaster.

Fig. 57. Caribbean map locating Martinique

Fig. 58. Plan of Fort-de-France, Martinique

Fort-de-France, the current capital of Martinique, is built in a half-circle around a small but deep harbor and accounts for one-third of the island's population. In addition to having a fine port, it is the island's commercial and cultural center. The town's focus is a twelve-and-a-half-acre waterfront park, Place de la Savane, a successful blend of sidewalk cafés, open spaces, tree-shaded footpaths, and well-trimmed gardens. A prominent feature of the park is a white marble statue of Empress Josephine, who was Martiniquan.

Although many of the streets of Fort-de-France are too narrow to accommodate the demands of contemporary automobiles, fortunately a good mix of commercial and residential occupancies in the downtown area provides an impressive cosmopolitan vitality.

The 1856 Gueydon Fountain, an interesting civic monument, was built to supply pure water to the capital. It required 28 months to construct and brought water from the heights of the Didier quarter of the city, a humid zone. The fountain no longer operates.

Fig. 59. Place de la Savane, city park in Fort-de-France, Martinique

Fig. 60. Statue of Empress Josephine, native of Martinique

Fig. 61. Gueydon Fountain, once the source of water for Fort-de-France, Martinique

Guadeloupe

Columbus named Guadeloupe in honor of the monks of the Monastery of Guadeloupe in Estremadura, in fulfillment of a vow he made to that group before starting out on his second voyage. The Spanish never colonized the island and finally abandoned it in 1604, because of the hostility of the Carib Indians. Although France claimed it in 1674, it was subsequently held by the British on three occasions, was transferred to Sweden in 1813, and finally was restored to France in 1816. Guadeloupe is really two islands, Basse Terre and Grande Terre, separated by a narrow channel.

Fig. 62. Caribbean map locating Guadeloupe

Fig. 63. Plan of Pointe-au-Pitre, Guadeloupe

Fig. 64. Place de la Victoire, waterfront park, Pointe-au-Pitre, Guadeloupe

The capital of Guadeloupe is Basse Terre, but the largest and most active town is Pointe-au-Pitre, because of its excellent deep-water harbor. Laid out with broad streets, Pointe-au-Pitre soon became the commercial center of the island, although it lacks the sophistication of Fort-de-France in Martinique. Considerable open area has been devoted to public space on the waterfront at Place de la Victoire, with a bandstand, fountains, benches, and recreation areas. A spacious marketplace, also with a fountain, is the scene of great activity on market days. A large segment of land in the newer section of town has been devoted to municipal buildings, including a Center for Arts and Culture.

St. Martin/Sint Maarten

The island owes its name to the day Columbus sailed into it, St. Martin's Day. Dutch and French settlers arrived in 1638 but two years later were driven out by the Spanish. In 1648, the French and Dutch regained possession and peaceably divided the island between them, with twenty-one square miles going to the French and sixteen square miles to the Dutch. This situation has endured, with only minor clashes, for almost 350 years.

Marigot is the capital of the French portion of the island. Less rugged than the south side of the island, this section continues to be used for farming and raising livestock.

Philipsburg, capital of the Dutch section, is located on a lagoon between the Great Salt Pond and Great Bay. It is a small two-street town with a long history of salt production for Holland's salt-fish industry until about 1900. The popularity of the town as a tourist center is reflected in its well-maintained pastel-colored buildings, attractive shops, and flower-bedecked streets.

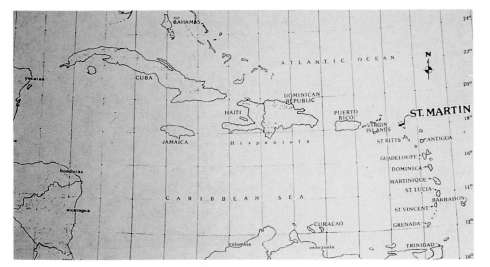

Fig. 65. Caribbean map locating St. Martin/Sint Maarten

THE FRENCH

ISLANDS

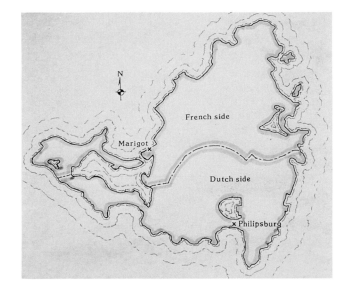

Fig. 66. Map of St. Martin/
Sint Maarten

Fig. 67. View of Marigot, capital of French St. Martin

OTHER ISLANDS
Curaçao

When Alonzo de Ojeda and Amerigo Vespucci visited Curaçao in 1499, it was occupied by Arawaks. The Spanish founded a small settlement there in 1527, which was taken over by the Dutch West India Company in 1634. Peter Stuyvesant, who was installed as governor in 1643, lost his leg leading an expedition against the island of St. Martin the following year. The French and the English made several attempts to occupy Curaçao; the English succeeded but returned the island to the Dutch in 1802 by the Treaty of Amiens. During the Napoleonic period, the British successfully attacked Curaçao in 1804–5 in their war against France and the Netherlands, but they again returned it to the Netherlands, this time in accordance with the Treaty of Paris in 1816.

The Dutch West India Company had been established in 1621 to facilitate settlements in the Caribbean. Because the Dutch came from a predominately urban society, their attitudes toward their colonial towns reflected their background, and their laws promoted the appearance of urban density. For example, corner lots had to be built up first to give the appearance of density. Lots that remained vacant could be confiscated and resold to buyers who would build. Mercantile advantage, rather than political or ecclesiastical promotion, was the main motivation of the Dutch settlers.

Curaçao is mostly flat, parched, and arid. Useless for agriculture, the island never became a labor-intensive plantation colony, although sheep, goats, cows, and horses were imported from Europe and raised here. It also became one of the most active slave centers in the Caribbean.

The capital of Curaçao is Willemstad, named for Dutch King Willem II in 1647. It is divided by St. Anna Bay, one section called Punda (the Point), and the other Otrobanda (the Other Side). The two sections are connected by the famous 100-year-old Queen Emma Floating Bridge. Built of wood in 1888, the structure was reworked in metal in 1939.

Fig. 68. Map of Caribbean locating Curaçao

Oil refining and tourism provide prosperity for Curaçao, and its historic structures are, for the most part, well preserved. Its pastel-colored buildings, with red tile roofs and curvilinear gables, maintain a Dutch flavor in Willemstad, earning for it the title "Amsterdam in Miniature."

Wilhelminaplein (Wilhelmina Park), with a statue of the Dutch queen of that name, is frequently the scene of cultural and musical events. A number of civic buildings face the park.

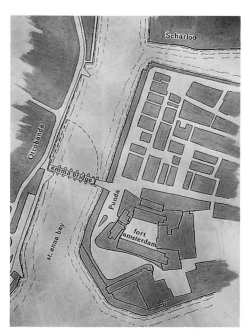

Fig. 69. Plan of Willemstad, Curaçao

Fig. 71. Wilhelmina Park, Willemstad, Curaçao

Fig. 70. Queen Emma Floating Bridge, Willemstad, Curaçao

U.S. Virgin Islands (the former Danish West Indies)

The Virgin Islands, lying between the Greater and the Lesser Antilles, were first settled by Amerindians who came to the area around 1500 B.C. Arawaks arrived there around A.D. 300. Columbus named the islands Las Virgenes, for St. Ursula and her martyred virgins. The islands remained undisturbed until 1555, when a Spanish expedition defeated the Caribs and claimed the islands. The Dutch tried to settle on St. Thomas in 1657 and the Danes in 1666. The British occupied St. Thomas in the years 1667–71, succeeded by the Danish West India Company in 1672. St. Croix was owned, successively, by the Dutch, English, Spanish, French, and the Knights of Malta; the last group sold it to the Danish West India Company in 1733. In 1755, the Danish crown took over the sovereign rights of the chartered company. The British again occupied the islands briefly, but they were returned to Denmark in 1817. When ships converted from sail power to steam, the Virgin Islands ceased to be an essential stopover point for shipping and the economy suffered. The emancipation of slaves and the decline in sugar prices had a similar effect on the plantations.

The United States purchased St. Thomas, St. Croix, St. John, and about fifty smaller islands from Denmark in 1917 because of their strategic value in protecting the approaches to the Panama Canal.

Charlotte Amalie, on St. Thomas, is the capital of the U.S. Virgin Islands, named in 1691 after the queen of Denmark. Its Government Hill district was planned in the 1760s as a regular grid of parallel and perpendicular streets, seemingly ignoring its steep terrain. As a result, a number of the streets actually developed as extended pedestrian staircases, and so they have remained.

Emancipation Park, on the waterfront in Charlotte Amalie, commemorates the 1848 abolition of slavery. Frequently the site of great community activity, the park offers a pavilion for concerts and other entertainment.

The island of St. Croix has two interesting towns, Christiansted and Frederiksted. The former, founded in 1735, was the capital of the Danish West

Fig. 72. Caribbean map locating the Virgin Islands

Fig. 73. Plan of Charlotte
Amalie, St. Thomas, U.S.
Virgin Islands

Fig. 74. Emancipation
Park, Charlotte Amalie,
St. Thomas, U.S.V.I.

Fig. 75. Waterfront Park, Christiansted, St. Croix, U.S.V.I.

Indies for many years and was one of the first Caribbean towns to adopt a building code. This 1747 document regulated street widths and block sizes and established zoning for the various occupancies. But, perhaps more important, buildings within the town had to use fire-resistant materials. This restriction prevented the fires that destroyed so much early architecture throughout the Caribbean, thus allowing one to see this port town much as it was in its earliest days.

The seventeenth- and eighteenth-century buildings in Christiansted have pleasant arcades over the sidewalks, providing good protection from sun and rain. The four square blocks along the waterfront have been designated a National Historic District, and the park adjacent to the fort is the scene of numerous community activities.

Frederiksted, founded by the Danes in 1751, has a deep-water harbor that became a major export site for rum and sugar. In 1867 a tidal wave washed away many of the town's buildings, and in 1878 fire resulting from a labor revolt destroyed many more. In the rebuilding, Frederiksted took on a Victorian appearance quite unlike the architecture of Christiansted, and the ornate Victorian style in vogue at that time is apparent in many of the replacement buildings.

CHAPTER 3

THE SUGAR
PLANTATION

Although other crops were grown in the Caribbean, sugar reigned supreme during colonial days and was the main reason for the competition among European powers for possession of the Caribbean islands. The nature of the operation required a large estate and a well-equipped factory to make cultivation profitable. In the eighteenth century, it was estimated that the minimum to accomplish this was 300 acres of land and 30 slaves to work it. Larger estates were even more profitable, and some were as large as 3,000 acres.

The original home of sugarcane was the South Pacific. Coming to Europe by way of India, it was probably introduced into Hispaniola by Columbus, and from there it went to the other islands. Barbados, in 1640, was the first English island to start systematic cultivation.

The desired ingredients for a sugar plantation were fertile soil, accessible location, proximity to shipping, and a stream of water on the premises. The principal buildings in the work area were the mill, boiling house, curing house, still, and trash house. In addition to the actual mill operation, there would have to be

Fig. 76. Old print showing slaves "holeing" sugarcane

workers' houses, and shops for the various crafts workers, such as blacksmiths, carpenters, coopers, and wheelwrights.

Demanding the least in terms of location was the animal mill, whose building was usually round or octagonal with a conical roof. At the center, three vertical rollers were rotated by a system of cogs, activated by one or two horizontal shafts to which oxen, horses, or mules were yoked. To power the mill, the animals were driven around in a continuous trot as the cane was fed into the rollers.

Fig. 77. Drawing of canes being carted to the mill, ca. 1836

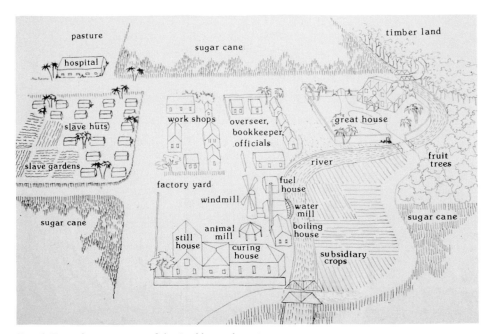

Fig. 78. Typical arrangement of the Caribbean plantation

For obvious reasons, if windmills were used to power a mill they had to be located on open or hilltop sites, which frequently restricted their use. Nevertheless, shells of this type of mill exist all over the Caribbean, attesting to its popularity.

Where available, streams or rivers provided the most efficient power, even when the water source was remote from the plantation. An elevated aqueduct was required for an overshot wheel, where the weight of the water turns the wheel; an undershot wheel depends upon the velocity of the water to turn it. Because the flow of a river or stream depends upon rainfall, dammed reservoirs were frequently created to store water in the event of a shortage. There are many aqueduct ruins in the Caribbean, some designed to bring water for a distance of

Fig. 79. Drawing of a Caribbean windmill, 1823

Fig. 80. Drawing showing operation of a windmill

Fig. 81. French illustration of an overshot water mill

several miles from the source. It was not unusual for two or all three of these power sources to be in use at a single plantation.

Steam power was introduced in the late eighteenth century but was not widely used in sugar mills until the second half of the nineteenth. This power change, which revolutionized the entire sugar industry, was accompanied by a change in the design of mill equipment, so that the rollers were placed horizontally instead of vertically.

Fig. 82. Hope Aqueduct, Kingston, Jamaica

Fig. 83. Drawing of an Antiguan boiling house, 1823

In the processing of sugar, the juice was squeezed from the cane and brought to the first cistern in the boiling house, where it was tempered with lime to assist in removing dirt. It was then boiled in a series of vats heated by furnaces fueled by bagasse, the crushed canes that had been dried in the trash house. When the juice was reduced to sugar, it was put into casks; they were moved to a curing house, then taken to the wharf and shipped. By the 1850s, decentralization was under way, for the cane increasingly was taken to remote factories to be processed.

Fig. 84. Whim Plantation great house, late 1700s, St. Croix, U.S. Virgin Islands

Fig. 85. Whim Plantation animal mill, St. Croix, U.S.V.I.

Fig. 86. Whim Plantation windmill, St. Croix, U.S.V.I.

Fig. 87. Whim Plantation windmill rollers

The "great house" of the planter was remote from the mill and slave quarters, usually in a location with the best view. By the early twentieth century, the planter-proprietor was frequently an absentee owner, and the overseer's house began to replace the great house.

The restoration at Whim Plantation, near Frederiksted in St. Croix, U.S. Virgin Islands, shows the typical organization of a Caribbean sugar mill. Whim is valuable as the only one preserved of some 300 estates on St. Croix operated by the Danes in the early 1700s (see plate 6). The site, 12 of the original 150 acres, is under the auspices of the St. Croix Landmarks Society. There is no stream to operate a water mill, but all other mill types are present. The floor of

Fig. 88. Whim Plantation steam
mill, St. Croix, U.S.V.I.

Fig. 89. Whim Plantation boiling house chimney
and windmill, St. Croix, U.S.V.I.

Fig. 90. Remains of Whim Plantation distillery,
St. Croix, U.S.V.I.

the animal mill is slightly elevated, accessible by ramp. Two animals rotated the
horizontal shaft that turned the central cylinder, which, with cogs, turned the
two exterior cylinders. This arrangement allowed cane to be fed in from both
sides. The windmill has been visually restored with excellent stone masonry, the
openings accented by classical quoins. Its floor is also elevated, although it is not
a two-level operation. The remains of two steam mills, put into use in 1865 after
emancipation, show that the rollers had been changed from vertical position to
horizontal, as was typical.

Only the foundation and great smokestack remain from the boiling house at
Whim, and a large copper still recalls the days of rum making. Whim Plantation
ceased its sugar mill operation in the 1920s. Its great house will be discussed later.

CHAPTER 4

THE SMALL RESIDENCE

The residence category is divided into three chapters for residences that are small, medium-sized, and large. The divisions are admittedly arbitrary, without specific areas, number of rooms, and so on, to determine the category. "Small residence" includes the most basic huts, chattel houses, one-story cottages, and bungalows.

GENERAL INFLUENCES

It is difficult to attribute with certainty the various external factors that influenced the design of the early small Caribbean residence, as African and European folk housing were similar in several basic ways. A two- or three-room rectangular house with mud walls and a thatched roof could have been found as easily in early rural England as in much of West Africa. We can speculate on certain design elements, however. The front porch can probably be attributed to African influence, as no antecedent is found in England or elsewhere in northern Europe. Living with constant tropical heat and humidity undoubtedly inspired this feature in African house design. Even though some parts of Central Africa have examples of gable-entry houses, the shotgun house (one room wide, one story tall, several rooms deep) was not used there. This organization of rooms is thought to have originated in the West Indies and, in the early nineteenth century, to have entered the United States via New Orleans.

SLAVE HUTS

Although some written descriptions of slave huts survive, helpful information comes from old prints that depict slave villages on plantations. Slave quarters were typically located where the soil was not tillable. Just large enough to house a slave household, one or two rooms, the square or rectangular huts were arranged in neat rows. They were built of materials most easily available and so varied considerably from place to place.

Sometimes slave huts were built by the planters, sometimes by the slaves themselves. The floor was usually tamped earth, with an occasional raised platform as a base for beds. We assume that wood and other tree products were the original materials for the walls. If timber was not available and local stone was, it would be used. Sometimes a timber frame would have an infill of stone or of wattle and daub. Wattle was a weaving of saplings, branches, vines, or split bamboo, over

Fig. 91. Print of a Caribbean plantation showing slave huts, 1784

which would be plastered a clay mixture (daub), a building technique with which the slaves were familiar because of its wide use in West Africa.

Palm thatch was a readily available roofing material that had been used by the Arawaks and Caribs, as well as by the Africans. Palm fronds were cut and left to become limp and flexible for easy handling. In Africa, long fronds were typically used, the two halves plaited together and attached horizontally to the roof purlins. The Caribbean method used fan-shaped palmetto fronds, which were laid up and down the roof. This method was probably used by the Arawaks, for Central American Indians, relatives of the Arawaks, still use it. Reeds, grass, or cane tops, in addition to palm fronds, were also used as roofing materials. Thatch was sometimes used for both roof and walls.

African huts tended to provide total closure against the outside, and it is not surprising that slaves refined this design. Their private world was confined to the interior of their huts, and they protected this limited privacy with solid walls or openings that could be closed with solid shutters. They cooked out of doors, as was customary in Africa. There were usually small garden plots around the huts, or provision grounds that the slaves tended in their free time. When they produced more than they needed for their own use, they frequently sold the surplus at Sunday market.

EMANCIPATION

Emancipation brought little immediate change to workers' dwellings. Wattle and daub, also thatch, survived into the twentieth century, and these materials continue to be used in some Caribbean localities. The use of wood boards has typically replaced wattle, however, and the use of unit masonry construction is now widespread. Probably the most important result of emancipation was the changed way in which the worker related to his home. Less need for isolation within the building allowed the development of a closer relationship to the land. And without restrictions imposed by the planter, individual creativity began to affect the buildings.

Mobile houses became desirable for a number of reasons. With the industrial cultivation of sugarcane, the demand for laborers was not locationally constant, and it sometimes became expedient to move the small dwellings according to need. Often these mobile homes were chattel houses, placed upon land that was not owned by the occupant.

The early-nineteenth-century invention of the light timber frame in the United States had considerable impact upon the entire West Indies. Modular construction was extremely useful, for it could be dismantled and moved easily. The invention of the fretsaw in the mid-nineteenth-century was responsible for much of the decorative delight of small Caribbean residences. A formal similarity can be observed in the small residences of the various Caribbean islands, yet a closer look reveals considerable variety, with no building characteristic common to all localities.

JAMAICA

Wattle and daub were widely used in constructing small residences in early Jamaica. Small flexible woods, such as wild coffee or split bamboo, were used to

Fig. 92. Old picture postcard showing thatch huts in Jamaica

weave the wattle panel, which was plastered over with clay or lime-and-earth mortar. The latter mixture was preferred, as it was more durable than clay.

Nog construction, a system using a wood framework with masonry infill, was also prevalent. In England, the word *nogging* specified brickwork set into a wood frame. In Jamaica, nogging (or nog) was a generic term, the masonry infill being

Fig. 93. Caribbean "mobile home" (chattel house)

Fig. 94. Veranda detail showing fretwork

Fig. 95. Bungalow, Black River, Jamaica

whatever material was available: brick, stone, or even concrete. *Spanish walling* was another name for stone nog, a term presumably retained from the use of this type of construction during the Spanish era.

In nog construction, an exterior coating—a mixture of one part lime to three parts earth—was usually applied over the posts and the infill. Whitewash, made from a mixture of white lime and water, was frequently the final finish to the wall. Blue color could be achieved by adding washing bluing; finely sieved red earth produced "red work"; the addition of yellow ochre produced "yellow work." Nog construction was not restricted to the small residence.

Postslavery days also saw the introduction of the bungalow to Jamaica, in its simplest version one or two rooms with a gabled roof. The gable end usually contained the main entrance, frequently with a veranda added. Plan shapes varied considerably, a T-shape being one favorite. This arrangement allowed a U-shaped veranda to wrap around the three sides of the front room of the house. Construction was usually wood frame raised on masonry piers. Much decorative variation occurred in the design of the veranda railing and in the fascia fretwork.

ST. KITTS

Small chattel houses were common in Basseterre, and moving the smaller ones to a new location only required providing four new piers. Gable or hip roofs, shingled walls, and windows with solid shutters were usually ingredients of these little buildings. Two-story buildings with living quarters above and commercial space below also occur in Basseterre.

Fig. 96. Small residences, Basseterre, St. Kitts

Fig. 97. Small residence, St. John's, Antigua

ANTIGUA

Some instances of "shipbuilding" construction—mortice-and-tenon joints with wooden pegs to provide the connections—are still found in Antigua. Small residences were frequently raised well off the ground by foundation walls, and typical Antiguan small residences had horizontal siding on a wood frame, corrugated iron hip roof, and windows with solid shutters.

ST. LUCIA

At one time, but no longer, the small St. Lucian residence was mobile; the house is still often raised above the ground on piers. Entry is on the long side, except in the villages, where the gable end may face the street and provide the doorway location.

BARBADOS

Because of close contacts with the North American colonies, Barbados was the first Caribbean island to make wide use of the modular dwelling that was developed in Boston. Its simplest version was one room, measuring three by six meters. Hip roofs gave way to gables, and the long side of the building faced the street. A pedimented entrance was flanked by one window on each side in a symmetrical arrangement. The solid shutters that were typical in other Caribbean locations were not used at the windows of Barbadian houses, although hoods were sometimes present, as were louvered shutters. Decoration, concentrated on the gable end, usually featured intricate fretwork and the use of color. Houses were enlarged by adding another similar module on an axis perpendicular to the street. Still others were added as needed.

GRENADA

The hillsides in St. George's, Grenada, are covered with small modular residences like the ones in Barbados (see plate 7). Set on pier foundations, these frame buildings used horizontal wood siding and gable roofs. Enlargement was usually by shed additions.

Fig. 98. Small residences, Castries, St. Lucia

TRINIDAD

Trinidad also used three-by-six-meter modular residences, sometimes supported by piers or by wood posts set in the ground. The gable roofs often had steeper slopes than were seen elsewhere in the Caribbean, and shed-roof additions were frequent. The Trinidadian love of elaborate fretwork was evidenced even in these

Fig. 99. Small residences, Bridgetown, Barbados

Fig. 100. Small residence, Port of Spain, Trinidad

small structures, and the street facade was symmetrical. Doors and windows were louvered for ventilation and had transoms above them.

BAHAMAS

After the British abolished the slave trade in 1807, the Royal Navy would capture slave ships sailing through Bahamian waters and free the Africans intended for slavery. Three communities were established for these people on New Providence Island, remote from Nassau, and the villages were similar to African settlements. However, people eventually shifted from these villages to locations closer to Nassau, primarily to an area south of town that became known as Grant's Town, after Major General Sir Lewis Grant. Picture postcards of this area from the early twentieth century show picturesque small stone or wood dwellings with thatched roofs. Some of the small frame houses were elevated for ventilation.

The thatched roofs are now gone from Grant's Town, but many reminders of the original settlement remain. The buildings stayed small but occurred in limitless variety. Although most are wood frame, stuccoed examples exist. Hip and gable roofs are covered with wood or asphalt shingles or with corrugated iron. The gables sometimes face the street, sometimes the side. Verandas are frequent; colors are vibrant. Many types of windows are in evidence, but some houses continue to use the traditional solid wood shutters to achieve closure of door and window openings. These small residences are an important part of Bahamian history.

Fig. 101. Old picture postcard, small residences in Grant's Town, Bahamas

PUERTO RICO

Early Spanish settlers in Puerto Rico inherited the small residence of the Taíno (Arawaks), which they changed from round, elliptical, or polygonal to rectangular. The term *bohío* was derived from the Taíno word for house and, in its simplest form, signified a two-room, timber-frame structure. The walls were constructed of cane or the inner bark of palm, and the roofs were thatch. The floor was usually packed earth or, if raised, was constructed of wood. Eventually

Fig. 102. Contemporary small residences, Grant's Town, Bahamas

Fig. 103. Small residences, Ponce, Puerto Rico

deemed inappropriate by the settlers, the bohíos were relegated to the lower class and the poor.

The three-by-three-meter module house probably came to Puerto Rico from Louisiana. It invited considerable variation, for the units could be placed lineally, or in a square, or in an L shape. The last arrangement was popular, with the open corner becoming a veranda. The usual construction for the wood-frame building was a foundation of masonry piers, horizontal siding, windows with solid shutters, and a gable roof.

CUBA

As in Puerto Rico, early small Cuban residences were influenced by bohíos (see plate 8). In rural areas, these modest hip-roof thatched structures may still be seen, although they are no longer typical. Frame buildings with horizontal wood siding became the norm for small residences. Verandas supported by wood posts were placed on one or several sides of the building, in response to climatic demands. Clay tile, available locally, was used on the hip, gable, or gabled-hip roofs. One-story frame row houses occurred in urban areas, located directly on the property lines, with *rejas* or solid shutters in the windows on the street side. These early row houses had high ceilings and sometimes opened onto courtyards at the rear.

DOMINICAN REPUBLIC

The most modest urban dwellings were wood frame with horizontal siding. Doors were usually solid, although they sometimes had louvers for ventilation.

Fig. 104. Row houses, Regla, Cuba

Fig. 105. Row houses, Santo Domingo, Dominican Republic

Individuality was achieved by color variation, and doors and trim were typically contrasting colors. In the congested areas of Santo Domingo, row houses usually had openings onto an interior courtyard as well as onto the street. More recent small residences have used stuccoed masonry.

HAITI

Many examples of vernacular small residences exist in Haiti, the poorest having walls of wattle daubed with mud and roofs of guinea grass or palm thatch. In some instances, particularly in kitchen areas, the daub was omitted, allowing for more positive ventilation. Packed-earth floors were sometimes covered with cement, and raised wood floors were also used. It is customary for the Haitian male to build a house when he intends to marry, even if it is only a single room (see plate 9). If more than one room was built, each room usually had its own entrance, provided with solid shutters or louvers. Color was important, even in the most modest structure, and decorative cutouts in wood provided an additional outlet for the designer's exuberance.

MARTINIQUE

Small Martiniquan residences were not mobile but were placed on carefully built foundations. A practice unique to Martinique was the use of two-foot-high masonry walls extending around the building, interrupted only by doors and by the structural corner wood posts, which were carried down to the foundation. Ship-building techniques traditionally provided the joinery for these wood structures. The residence facades were usually painted a light color, with contrasting colors on the low masonry band and on the doors. White was rarely used, except in city houses. Closure at the openings was accomplished by solid or louvered shutters. In the early houses, thatch was sometimes used as the roofing material, but tile was also popular.

Fig. 106. Wattle and thatch dwelling, rural Haiti

Fig. 107. Small urban residences, Fort-de-France, Martinique

GUADELOUPE

Although Guadeloupe also maintained a shipbuilding tradition in house construction, site preparation was entirely unlike Martinique's. The structure often sat directly on the ground or, on occasion, atop rocks placed under each corner or wood posts embedded in the ground. The important thing was to maintain mobility. When it was time to move, the entire small building was loaded onto a truck and transported to the new site. Prefabricated units three by three meters, probably imported from the United States, were popular. If these units were used to enlarge a dwelling, it was important not to destroy the mobility of the structure. Wood siding and wood shingles were the traditional wall-covering materials, although sheet metal has become popular. The number of masonry residences is also steadily increasing. Color and decoration have always been important considerations in the Guadeloupe residence (see plate 10).

ST. MARTIN/SINT MAARTEN

The general architectural differences between the two sections of the island are not apparent in small residences. More well-maintained small residences are in evidence in Dutch Philipsburg than in French Marigot, perhaps because the Dutch have successfully adapted many small dwellings to tourist shops. In both countries, the typical small residence is frame with horizontal wood siding or shingles and a hip roof surfaced with corrugated iron. Solid shutters protect door and window openings, and a veranda may occur at the entrance. The small residences in Sint Maarten are generally more colorful than those of their French neighbors.

Fig. 108. Small residence, Marigot, St. Martin

Fig. 109. Small residence, Philipsburg, Sint Maarten

Fig. 110. Small residence, Scharloo section of Willemstad, Curaçao

CURAÇAO

Although Curaçao is famous for its gables, its small freestanding residences were frequently built with hip roofs and no overhangs and surfaced with corrugated iron. Wall construction was usually wood frame with horizontal siding. The entrance was on the long side, with no portico to provide entry protection. Solid

Fig. III. Urban residence, Christiansted, St. Croix, U.S. Virgin Islands

wood shutters occurred at windows and doors. Urban residences were usually one-story, gable-roof row houses, also with shuttered doors and windows. Parapeted gables, tile roofs, and dormers gave these a Dutch flavor (see plate 11).

U.S. VIRGIN ISLANDS

An 1848 description of a plantation near Frederiksted, St. Croix, mentions a "negro village of neat little stone houses covered with shingles." This construction was not usual, however; from early times, small residences were simple wood-frame structures with shingled or clapboard walls. They were raised off the ground, and in urban locations masonry steps to the entry were typically supported by arches over the gutters in front of the house. Roofs were usually hipped, although gables were occasionally used. Door and window openings were closed with solid wood shutters.

If space permitted, a porch with shed roof was sometimes added to the front of the house. It was there that individuality frequently manifested itself in the design of fretwork. Color choice for the residence was also an important consideration.

Small residences of this description are still scattered throughout the U.S. Virgin Islands, although jalousied windows have frequently been placed in the shuttered openings.

CHAPTER 5

THE MEDIUM-SIZED RESIDENCE

The medium-sized residence is the middle- and upper-middle-class residence of the Caribbean. These houses, frequently two stories high, are comfortable and spacious but not luxurious. Many of the best truly Caribbean expressions of residential architecture fall in this category.

JAMAICA

Falmouth, in Trelawny Parish, is referred to as Jamaica's "Georgian" town. It was the fashionable location in the eighteenth century for the fine townhouses of wealthy planters. House plans, as well as details of doors, windows, staircases, and cornices, were taken from pattern books produced in England.

The Edward Barrett House was built by the wealthy owner of Cinnamon Hill Plantation in 1799 on Market Street in Falmouth. An open colonnade supports the overhanging second floor. The lower part of the house is cut stone, with wood frame construction above. Wrought-iron railings originally occurred on all of the second-story triple-hung windows, with interior folding louver shutters for privacy. Adam-style detailing was used extensively on the interior.

The Town House, on Church Street in Montego Bay, is an eighteenth-century Georgian house whose design now completely denies its location in the tropics. It has experienced a variety of tenants. For a time, it was a small hotel; then a synagogue occupied its second floor. For the next fifty years it was a Masonic lodge. A complete restoration in 1967 removed the wooden veranda added in an attempt to suit the building to the Jamaican climate. The stucco was also removed at that time, exposing the original red brick and white stone quoins. The lower level now houses a restaurant.

The Althenheim House, on King Street in Spanish Town, was built about 1760. It has Flemish bond brickwork, with dentil stringcourse and a parapet with coping and dentils. Pedimented coolers were added at the windows when these came into fashion in the mid-nineteenth century. The house is a good example of Georgian, with a rectangular plan and a formal and symmetrical front facade. A pedimented portico protects the entrance. The building now serves as a secretarial school.

Fig. 112. Barrett House, 1799, in Falmouth, the "Georgian" town of Jamaica

Fig. 113. The Town House, Montego Bay, Jamaica, eighteenth-century Georgian

An eighteenth-century house on White Church Street, Spanish Town, has a major central hipped section, with projections front and rear. The brick is laid up in Flemish bond, and wood shingles are used on the roof. Entrance is through a walled garden. Hoods protect the windows on the south side. The symmetrical front elevation has jalousies in combination with sliding-sash windows.

Fig. 114. Georgian-style Althenheim House, ca. 1760, Spanish
Town, Jamaica

Fig. 115. Eighteenth-century house on White Church Street, Spanish Town, Jamaica

Fig. 116. Invercauld, 1894, Black River, Jamaica, typical turn of the century wealthy merchant's home

Fig. 117. Presbytery, Basseterre, St. Kitts

Invercauld, built in Black River in 1894, was typical of the elegant turn-of-the-century waterfront homes built on High Street by well-to-do merchants. This timber structure was assembled primarily from precut components shipped onto the island. Its design included decorative gables, bay windows, intricate fretwork, balusters, and coolers. The house fell into serious disrepair but was rescued in an adaptive-use restoration in 1990 that added wings and turned it into a guest house.

ST. KITTS

The Georgian House Restaurant, Basseterre, originally an eighteenth-century residence, is symmetrical except for the arched doorway on the left of the front facade (see plate 12). A central Palladian window occurs on the upper level, with a broken pediment above the first-floor entrance. Sidelights, a transom, and a fanlight grace the entrance. The house has a hip roof, stone stringcourse, flush quoins, and flat arches at the windows.

One of the most handsome residences in Basseterre is the Presbytery, next to the Roman Catholic Co-Cathedral. The house has a hip roof with a nine-bay upper veranda that relates to the five unequal bays of the lower level. The ground level is constructed of stone, the upper portion of horizontal siding on wood frame.

ANTIGUA

St. John's has a number of residences that resemble the Georgian architecture built along the Atlantic coastline in the North American colonies in the mid-eighteenth century. Familiar ingredients are the hip roof; two-story, wood-frame construction; and formal front facade, symmetrical about a central entrance. The double-hung windows have louvered shutters.

BARBADOS

A number of Dutch sugar planters came to Barbados in the mid-seventeenth century. The Nicholls Building, about 1700, is probably the oldest surviving townhouse in Bridgetown, and its distinctive curvilinear gables indicate its Dutch heritage. Stone quoins occur at its corners.

Fig. 118. "Caribbean Georgian" residence, St. John's, Antigua

Fig. 119. Nicholls Building, ca. 1700, probably the oldest townhouse in Bridgetown, Barbados

Fig. 120. Townhouses, Bay Street, Bridgetown, Barbados, with unique Barbadian urban characteristics

Fig. 121. The Grotto, typical Bridgetown, Barbados, suburban house, built in the second half of the nineteenth century

Characteristics unique to Barbadian urban architecture can be seen on two interesting townhouses, Lynton and Carlisle View, on Bay Street in Bridgetown. The corners of the buildings are rounded, and in front elevation, the parapets, with their concave curves at the ends, have been given the name "Barbadian parapets" and are reputed to provide protection to the roof during high winds. Their curves relate somewhat to the side rooflines of the projecting verandas below. Lynton and Carlisle View reportedly were built by sea captains at mid-nineteenth century.

The Grotto, on River Road in Bridgetown, was built in the second half of the nineteenth century and is typical of suburban houses of this era in and around the town. It is symmetrical, with double stairs leading to the main upper level. A single Demarara shutter is attached to the bottom of the pediment of the portico and at the windows on the sides of the house.

Villa Franca, in Hastings, another symmetrical residence, has an elaborate double stair to a landing, then a single stair to the entrance portico (see plate 13). Above the arcaded lower veranda is a front gallery enclosed by jalousies and sash windows. The parapet along the front edge of the hip roof does not have the concave curves of the Barbadian parapet.

GRENADA

Because Grenada was alternately a colony of Britain and of France, its architecture is a blend of both traditions. Many existing fish-scale tile roofs and ornate iron balconies attest to the persistence of the French tradition.

Fig. 122. Sedan porch
residences (on the left),
used in the seventeenth
and eighteenth centuries
in St. George's, Grenada

During the seventeenth and eighteenth centuries, sedan porches were built at the fronts of residences to shelter passengers embarking or disembarking from sedan chairs, a frequently used mode of transport at the time. The sheltered entry of sedan chairs was accomplished by leaving the porches open on either side.

TRINIDAD

George Brown, who came from Scotland in 1883, was responsible for much of the rebuilding required after the disastrous Port of Spain fire in 1895. His introduction of the cast-iron frame to shops on Frederick Street transformed the character of this part of town. He also mass produced fretwork and other building ornaments that became popular in residential construction. His own house, on Queen's Park West, is refrained symmetry with embellishments, including metal cresting and pinnacles. Brown went back to Scotland in 1921.

The Boissiere House, also on Queen's Park West, Port of Spain, was designed by Edward Bowen and built in 1904 for the owners of large cocoa plantations (see plate 14). Its heavy ornamentation disguises its relatively simple concrete-block construction. The steeply pitched roof is covered with green slate, and the

Fig. 123. Early twentieth-century home of architect George Brown, Port of Spain, Trinidad

Fig. 124. French influence, Port of Spain, Trinidad

large dormer gable is one of Trinidad's finest examples of fretwork. An entire
Chinese pavilion is included in one of the projecting galleries.

At the corner of Oxford Street and St. Vincent, in Port of Spain, a house with
a mansard roof and dormers is an example of French influence in Trinidad. This
suburban residence has a veranda on two sides, with a pedimented portico at the
entrance.

Fig. 125. Typical medium-sized residence, Port of Spain, Trinidad

A residence on Gordon Street, Port of Spain, demonstrates several details typical of many Trinidad residences. The two symmetrical projecting "bay window" forms continue up to the eaves of gable roofs whose slopes become more shallow at the point of overhang. Brackets help accomplish this somewhat complicated juncture of walls and roof. The projecting isolated central entrance portico, with considerable ornamentation, is of shallower slope than the major gables but also has a still shallower slope for its overhang. Pinnacles adorn the ridge points of the gables.

BAHAMAS

The Deanery, about 1710, on Cumberland Street in Nassau, is probably the oldest residence in the Bahamas (see plate 15). The latticed verandas on the street (east) side are its most dominant design characteristic, and in the original design these occurred on the north and west elevations as well. The roof is a square hip, wood shingled, with a cupola. A separate building contains the kitchen, with its fireplace and domed brick oven. The outhouse known as the "Slaves' Quarters" has, on its north and west elevations, loopholes in lieu of windows.

Balcony House, on Market Street in Nassau, is a two-story frame house built of American soft cedar, ca. 1790. Its careful detailing indicates that it was probably built by ships' carpenters. The second-floor balcony, which overhangs the street, is supported by wooden "knees." The street elevation is asymmetrical, with clapboard siding and shuttered windows. An interior staircase is believed to have been taken from a ship. There are a number of outbuildings on the property.

Magna Carta Court is outstanding as one of the few exposed-stone houses in Nassau, and its surfaces may have originally been stuccoed. The street facades are without decoration, and the roof is a simple hip. Flat arches are employed over the window openings, which have hinged shutters at the sides. This house reverses the typical arrangement and places the wall of wood louvers on the rear of the building instead of on the street side.

Fig. 126. Balcony House, ca. 1790, Nassau, Bahamas, with detailing by ships' carpenters

Fig. 127. Magna Carta Court, one of the few exposed-stone houses in Nassau, Bahamas

PUERTO RICO

Residences in Old San Juan are completely urban in character, constructed right to the sidewalk, frequently with shops at ground level. The upper levels were related to the street activity via handsome iron or wood balconies. Door and window openings on the street facade were trimmed with rather severe mouldings, usually painted white. Colonnades or arcades surrounded the inner courtyards, where family activities took place.

Fig. 128. Rear of Magna Carta Court

Fig. 129. Typical townhouses, Old San Juan, Puerto Rico

The charm of Ponce is quite different from that of Old San Juan. In 1820, a fire destroyed most of the town, and the governor ordered that the rebuilt houses be set farther apart, making the town much less congested than San Juan. Ponce is well known for its single-family homes, which present delightful individuality and high style even when modest in scale, a combination of rococo and neoclassicism.

Font-Ubides (Monsanto) Mansion, 1912, on Calle Villa in Ponce, has delicate detailing and the typical raised floor level, with twin projecting round porches whose roofs are supported by Corinthian columns (see plate 16). Arch-headed doorways lead into the residence.

Villaronga, also built in 1912 in Ponce, was the home and studio of architect Alfredo B. Weichers. Its most eye-catching detail is the open round colonnade on the roof. An ornate parapet, swags, and various reliefs ornament this neoclassical building.

CUBA

Old Havana has changed little for centuries and was classified as a world heritage site by UNESCO in 1982. As in Puerto Rico, the Spanish colonists in Havana constructed their homes around lushly planted central patios.

House of the Arabs is a typical sixteenth-century, two-story urban house whose street elevation is plain except for a second-floor wood balcony extending the length of the building. Matching wood *rejas* protect the windows at street level. The interior courtyard is surrounded by a second-floor balcony onto which the rooms open. A grapevine trellis filters the sunlight into this area. One room in the House of the Arabs serves as Havana's only mosque.

The little town of San Miguel has a good collection of one-story, wood-frame residences, typically with high ceilings, raised floors, and generous wrap-around porches. The low-sloping roofs are covered with red tile.

Similar houses are found in Varadero, on the north coast. This small town became a popular resort area at the turn of the century, and many substantial medium-sized residences were constructed here at that time.

Fig. 130. House of the Arabs, typical sixteenth-century two-story urban house, Havana, Cuba

Fig. 131. Interior courtyard, House of the Arabs

Fig. 132. Typical one-story, wood-frame residence, San Miguel, Cuba

Fig. 133. Typical residence design, Varadero, Cuba

Fig. 134. Two-story beach house, Varadero, Cuba

DOMINICAN REPUBLIC

Tostado House, in Santo Domingo, was built in the sixteenth century for Francisco del Tostado, the first native professor at the first university in the New World, who lived here until he was killed by one of the bombs thrown by Drake's British troops in 1586. One of the last two-story residences built in Old Santo Domingo, it is a composition in stone, brick, and stucco, with unexpected Gothic tracery in an opening above the entrance. The subsequent advent of one-

Fig. 135. Tostado House, sixteenth century, one of the last two-story residences built in Old Santo Domingo, Dominican Republic

Fig. 136. Typical mixed-occupancy urban building, Santo Domingo, Dominican Republic

story residences here may have resulted from a decline in urban population, which led to a land surplus. Tostado House now houses a museum.

Later Santo Domingo has a number of two-story buildings that accommodate housing on the upper level above commercial spaces at street level. Generous doors from the residential spaces open onto upper balconies, and the buildings are frequently embellished with Spanish Renaissance details.

HAITI

In the scorched-earth military strategy employed in Haiti's struggle for independence, most of the island's eighteenth-century architecture was destroyed. Much delightful and unusual turn-of-the-century residential architecture in Port-au-Prince, however, dates from 1880 to 1920 and demonstrates amazing imagination and fancy, primarily in unexpected roof forms dominated by steeply sloped "spires." This architecture is thought to have resulted from the influence of the Paris Colonial Exposition of 1890, where pavilions and pagodas from the East Indies were on exhibition. Corrugated iron is currently the usual roof material, although some examples of slate roofs still exist. Building construction is frequently brick nog, with complicated placement of the half-timber elements. Roof overhangs and balconies are supported by wood brackets, and ornamental turned wood and fretwork occur often. Solid shutters typically provide closure at the windows.

Fig. 137. House on Avenue J. B. Lalue, Port-au-Prince, Haiti

Fig. 138. Typical turn-of-the-century urban residence, Port-au-Prince, Haiti

Mixed occupancy is also a characteristic of congested urban areas in Haiti, where residential units occur above commercial spaces. Living areas open onto upper balconies, and solid shutters are provided to cover all openings.

Fig. 139. Medium-sized residence, Port-au-Prince, Haiti

Fig. 140. Mixed-occupancy urban building, Cap Haïtien, Haiti

MARTINIQUE

Some two-story frame residences in Fort-de-France use the two-foot-high masonry band at the base familiar as the norm in small one-story frame residences. Tile roofs continue to be commonplace throughout the city, and door and window openings are covered by louvered shutters.

There is continued strong French influence in Martiniquan buildings, with many mansard or gambrel roofs with dormers. Downtown commercial occupancies usually have one or two residential floors above. In masonry structures, segmental arches are frequently used above door and window openings.

Fig. 141. Two-story urban residence, Fort-de-France, Martinique

Fig. 142. French influence in a townhouse, Fort-de-France, Martinique

GUADELOUPE

The dominant occupancy pattern in downtown Pointe-au-Pitre is commercial at street level and residential on the levels above, with solid shutters over the openings at all levels. Although cast-iron balconies and roof dormers are frequent, French influence seems much less here than in Fort-de-France, partly owing to the scarcity of red tile roofs in Guadeloupe.

Fig. 143. Townhouse, Pointe-au-Pitre, Guadeloupe

Fig. 144. Schoelcher Museum, formerly a residence, Pointe-au-Pitre, Guadeloupe, demonstrating French classicism

Fig. 145. Residence converted to the Herminier Museum, Pointe-au-Pitre, Guadeloupe, with cast-iron construction

The Schoelcher Museum, formerly a residence, is one of the few examples of French classicism in Pointe-au-Pitre. Rusticated pilasters occur at the lower level, and above the central stringcourse fluted pilasters support another stringcourse above. Cast-iron balconies and applied swags ornament the facade. Above the classical entablature is an inappropriate corrugated iron roof.

The Herminier Museum, another converted residence, is one of many examples of cast-iron construction in the French Antilles. The five-bay masonry facade has pilasters at the corners and flanking each of the segmental-arch openings. Ornamental cast-iron railings and sheet-metal fascia contrast with the sedate facade. This is one of the few remaining examples of tile roofs in Pointe-au-Pitre.

ST. MARTIN

A townhouse in Marigot was constructed of rubble stone, with the main level elevated six steps above the sidewalk. A projecting second-floor balcony is supported by five scroll-shaped iron brackets. Wood fretwork adorns the balcony and the fascia, and solid shutters protect all openings. The unusual four-bay front facade relates awkwardly to the six bays of the balcony.

CURAÇAO

Merchants built the original buildings in the Punda section of Willemstad, with warehouse storage at ground level and residential space above. The typical arrangement was a gabled roof with curvilinear or truncated gable over the main area, and on the street facade an open gallery covered by a flat roof supported by a colonnade or arcade. As more living space was needed, part or all of the gallery

Fig. 146. Townhouse, Marigot, St. Martin

Fig. 147. Typical expansion of townhouse in Willemstad, Curaçao

Fig. 148. Revised townhouse, Willemstad, Curaçao

Fig. 149. Hotel Caracas, Scharloo, Curaçao, stressing classicism

Fig. 150. Central Historic Archives, Scharloo, Curaçao, showing South American influence in an adapted residence

was enclosed. Eventually, about the middle of the eighteenth century, frequently the galleries not only were fully enclosed but were incorporated into the facade. In some instances, a gable roof was added above what had been a flat roof. If the original gable was retained, two gables would exist, not necessarily of the same design as the later ones tended to be plainer, or even classical pediments.

When Punda became a shopping area, the major change was that the ground-level warehouse space became shops, while in most instances the upper portion continued to serve as residential space. The delightful assortment of pastel colors on these buildings is attributed to an 1817 ordinance that forbade white exterior walls because of the glare they produced.

In the 1850s, expansion in Willemstad occurred primarily to the east, across the canal into the suburb of Scharloo. Houses here reflected a greater interest in classical detailing than did the buildings in Punda and Otrobanda. Hotel Caracas, in Scharloo, was originally the residence of Luis Brion, the commander-in-chief of the Venezuelan army who in 1805 drove away the English who were attacking Curaçao. The house is highly classical, with a dominant pedimented entrance portico supported by four pseudo-Doric columns. The elevated main floor is approached by a monumental axial stairway. A Doric entablature surrounds the building, and a hipped tile roof rises above the triglyphs and metopes of the entablature.

Eventually, in Scharloo, some houses showed South American influence, the ornate *vermicelli* style. One such residence now houses the Central Historic Archives. It is fronted by a seven-bay arcade topped with urns and a balustrade. Applied decoration ornaments the windows and doors, and boldly contrasting colors emphasize the ornamentation.

U.S. VIRGIN ISLANDS

The Bornn House, about 1827 on Norre Gade in Charlotte Amalie, is a rectangular masonry house with hip roof, its main level elevated well above the street with a bracketed cast-iron balcony projecting from the second floor facing the street. Quoins emphasize the corners, and an intermediate stringcourse occurs

Fig. 151. Bornn House, ca. 1827, Charlotte Amalie, St. Thomas, U.S. Virgin Islands

only on the street elevation. At the windows, solid shutters swing out and lou-vered shutters swing in. Exterior doors are also protected by solid shutters.

The 1854 Yellow Brick Building, on Government Hill, is typical of many late-nineteenth-century houses in Charlotte Amalie with a restrained five-bay front facade and hip roof. Brick flat arches span the window and door openings, where solid shutters provide cover. A three-bay bracketed cast-iron upper bal-cony embellishes the street facade.

The former Anglican Rectory, about 1860, also on Government Hill, is a simple brick rectangle to which have been attached highly ornamented cast-iron galleries and stairs. Arcades have been attached between the slender columns, made of sheet metal at the upper gallery and cast iron below. The cast-iron rail-ings are of different designs on the two levels. Solid shutters protect the windows and exterior doors. The building now operates as a guest house and restaurant.

Fig. 152. Yellow Brick Building, 1854, typical late-nineteenth-century house in Charlotte Amalie, St. Thomas, U.S.V.I.

Fig. 153. Former Anglican Rectory, ca. 1860, Charlotte Amalie, St. Thomas, U.S.V.I., with much ornament on a simple rectangle

CHAPTER 6

THE LARGE RESIDENCE

Large residences, which usually belonged to planters, owners of estates, wealthy merchants, and government officials, often reflected European and eclectic influences.

JAMAICA

Headquarters House, built about 1755, is the sole survivor of four houses built at the same time by wealthy Kingston merchants. Originally the home of Thomas Hibbert the Eldest, its later occupancies connect it closely with the history of Jamaica. In 1814, it was purchased by the War Office to be the official residence of the general of the army, giving it its current name. From this house, General Sir Willoughby Cotton dealt with the Christmas Rebellion of 1831, and Major-General Luke Smythe O'Connor agonized over the 1865 Morant Bay Uprising. In 1872, when the capital was moved from Spanish Town to Kingston, Headquarters House became the office of the colonial secretary. After independence, the Jamaica legislature met here until 1960, when it moved into the new Gordon House.

Built of brick, stone, and timber, the house consists of a basement, ground

Fig. 154. Headquarters House, ca. 1755, Kingston, Jamaica, originally a residence, has experienced a number of significant governmental occupancies

floor, upper floor, and attic. Its front elevation is symmetrical, with three pedimented gables. Engaged columns are placed on the lower piers and on the upper facade. An outstanding interior feature is the mahogany stairway connecting the two main floors. Most of the original woodwork also remains in the doors, frames, wainscot, and moldings.

Rose Hall great house, in St. James Parish, was built about 1770, one of the largest plantation houses in Jamaica. Its Renaissance formality is created by an exterior grand double stairway leading to a spacious balustraded terrace and wings that extend from either side of the main rectangle, originally terminating in identical end pavilions that have since been removed. The central arch-headed entry is flanked by engaged Tuscan columns and entablature.

An arcaded basement supports a main level built of well-executed cutstone and an upper level of smooth-finished stucco with corner quoins. Unoccupied for years, the house suffered from deterioration and vandals until it was finally restored in the late 1960s. It is now maintained by the Georgian Society of Jamaica.

Devon House, built in Kingston in 1881, was the home of George Stiebel, who had made his fortune mining gold in Venezuela. This property had previously been the site of a house known as Devon Pen, and some outbuildings from that era remain. The mansion is brick covered with wood and, although Georgian in appearance, designed for the tropics. What appear to be shutters flanking the double-hung windows are actually louvers opening into the rooms. Generous verandas with balustraded decks above occur on all sides of the house. The ceilings are high, and interior detailing is meticulous, with well-designed mahogany staircases, paneling, and doorways. The house was bought by the Jamaican government in 1967, restored, and appropriately furnished. A bar, restaurants, and shops now cater to an active tourist trade.

The King's House property, in St. Andrew Parish, was originally known as

Fig. 155. Rose Hall great house, ca. 1770, St. James Parish, Jamaica, Renaissance formality in the Caribbean

Fig. 156. Entrance, Rose Hall

Fig. 157. Devon House, 1881, Kingston, Jamaica, Georgian with tropical features

Fig. 158. King's House, St. Andrew Parish, Jamaica, buttressed replacement of the original residence destroyed in the 1907 earthquake

Sumerset Pen and comprised 170 acres of land. At first the Bishop's Lodge, it became the home of colonial governors in 1872. The residence was destroyed in the 1907 earthquake, and its replacement, with its flying buttresses, seems preoccupied with surviving natural disasters.

ST. KITTS

The French governor of St. Kitts for twenty-one years, M. Phillipe de Langvilliers de Poincy, in 1642, built an enormous square house of red brick and cut stone named La Fontaine in the hills overlooking Basseterre. It stood in a walled formal garden, with terraced levels connected by monumental stairs. In its finished state, it was as if the Louis XIII style had been transplanted into the Caribbean. An amateur botanist, de Poincy imported many exotic plants to beautify his estate, including the poinciana tree reputedly named for him. After the governor's death, the great house was severely damaged during an earthquake in 1689. No attempt was made to reconstruct it, and its ruins were pilfered for material for other buildings. Little remains except a grotto and portions of terracing and stairs.

Most of the St. Kitts estate houses have disappeared. Among the few that have been saved is Fairview, dating to the early 1700s. Allowed to fall into severe disrepair during the nineteenth century, in the 1960s it was restored and adapted for use as the core of a small hotel. It is restrained in design, with a continuous veranda on the lower level and an open balcony above.

Government House is a good example of British tropical colonial architecture. Although built as a rectory, it has been the official residence of the governor general since 1882. A generous veranda wraps the building at ground level, and a projecting pedimented porch at the upper level defines the central entry. Solid shutters protect the windows.

The numbers of Roman Catholic Irish who migrated to St. Kitts as indentured servants caused concern on the part of the English, who feared that in event of war with France they might side with the Catholic French. For this reason, Roman Catholicism was forbidden in St. Kitts for a period, and a cupola on a

Fig. 159. Old print of the estate of M. Phillipe de Langvilliers de Poincy, St. Kitts, showing Louis XIII style transplanted to the Caribbean

building during those years marked it as a haven for Roman Catholics. A prominent house on Liverpool Row is one of several such buildings still in existence in Basseterre. Its commercial lower floor is arcaded stone with prominent imposts, keystones, and stringcourse. The keystones interrupt what would have been pointed arches. Horizontal wood siding occurs on the wood-frame upper floor, along with shuttered windows.

Fig. 160. Fairview, early 1700s residence restored and adapted for use as a hotel

Fig. 161. Government House, Basseterre, St. Kitts, British tropical colonial architecture

Fig. 162. House on Liverpool Row, Basseterre, St. Kitts, with a cupola that secretly indicated a haven for Roman Catholics

ANTIGUA

Clarence House was built in 1787 as a birthday gift for Prince William Henry, Duke of Clarence, who was to become King William IV of England. The house is now the official country residence of the governor general of Antigua. A tripartite roof covers a square floor plan surrounded by verandas, on which shutters offer privacy. The building is elevated on a stone foundation with arched openings, with a double exterior stairway leading to the main entrance. The interior is marked by a sense of openness throughout, with excellent architectural detailing, particularly in the woodwork.

Fig. 163. Clarence House, Antigua, country residence of the governor general

Fig. 164. The Admiral's House, Nelson's Dockyard, Antigua, with attentiveness to tropical demands

When the sugar industry in Antigua collapsed in the middle of the nineteenth century, most of the estate houses were abandoned and left to decay or were pulled down. A fortunate exception is the Weatherhills great house, built in 1890. The estate dates from 1660, when the original crop was cotton, followed by sugarcane. The entrance portico and the shuttered windows of the house are English in origin, but the tripartite hip roof and the long veranda with its fretwork fascia are Caribbean.

The Admiral's House, at Nelson's Dockyard, was occupied by Horatio Nelson from 1786 to 1787. The two-story, wood-frame residence has horizontal siding, raised on a stone foundation, and a bipartite wood-shingle hip roof extending out over two-story verandas that wrap around three sides of the building. Solid wood shutters protect the windows. The design shows true attentiveness to tropical demands, unlike those of most of the buildings at Nelson's Dockyard. The Admiral's House now functions as a museum.

ST. LUCIA

St. Lucia's Government House is located two-thirds of the way up Morne Fortuné (Hill of Good Luck) in Castries, looking out over the Caribbean Sea. Its architecture is an eclectic combination of details: rubble stonework with quoins, Palladian windows, stringcourses, ornamental cast iron. Its badge of royal connection appears on the dominant tower, whose top is literally crowned. The elaboration of the tower and the lower level contrast with the plainness of the basic upper structure, which on the main elevation is relieved only by Demarara

Fig. 165. Government House, Castries, St. Lucia, an example of eclectic Caribbean colonial

shutters at the windows. A variety of additional unrelated architectural details occurs on the end elevations.

BARBADOS

Interesting architectural ties had early been established between Barbados and the Carolina colony in North America as a result of the involvement of Barbadian planters in establishing the settlement Charles Towne, later Charleston. Eventually, there were to be seven colonial governors of Carolina who were Barbadian or of direct Barbadian descent. Grand Carolina houses, such as Middleton Place and Drayton Hall, were built by these settlers. The most prevalent example of Barbadian influence, however, was the "single house" design that was brought to Carolina. These long, one-room-deep houses fit perfectly Charleston's long, narrow house lots, an arrangement that also allowed for positive ventilation between houses. Because of the many disastrous fires in Bridgetown, few of these single houses remain in Barbados; Charleston, South Carolina, is full of them.

It is claimed that only three Jacobean houses exist on the North American continent and that two of these are in Barbados. The best known is St. Nicholas Abbey, about 1660, an English transplant complete with chimneys and even fireplaces. The house has three stories, curvilinear gables with tall finials, and elaborate quoins. The facades are original, except for the eighteenth-century entry porch of three Roman arches.

Drax Hall Plantation, in St. George Parish, was one of the earliest and biggest sugar properties in Barbados. This Jacobean great house was built about 1650,

Fig. 166. "Single house," Charleston, South
Carolina, showing architectural influence
from Barbados

Fig. 167. St. Nicholas Abbey, ca. 1660, St. Peter Parish, Barbados, Jacobean in the Caribbean

and its stuccoed walls, steep gables with parapets, and corner finials very much
resemble the details of mansions being built in England at that time. The addition of Demarara half-shutters provides a tropical flavor.

The original design of Sam Lord's Castle, in St. Philip Parish, about 1820, was
restrained classicism with little ornamentation except for plaster "eyebrows"
above the lower-level windows, decorative recessed panels, and a rusticated basement. The castellations on the parapet were added later by Lord. Good wood and
plaster detailing enhance the interior. The building is now a hotel.

Fig. 168. Drax Hall, ca. 1650, St. George Parish, Barbados, another Jacobean example

Fig. 169. Sam Lord's Castle, ca. 1820, St. Philip Parish, Barbados, with medieval details added to restrained classicism

Fig. 170. Villa Nova, 1834, St. John Parish, Barbados, showing unique Barbadian details

Villa Nova was originally a 1,000-acre sugar plantation built in 1834 of quarried white coral limestone, a porous stone with good insulating qualities. An extensive one-story veranda with latticed arcade wraps around the building. The entrance is emphasized by an unusual pedimented portico. A stringcourse occurs two feet below the parapet, a detail seen frequently in Barbados. Half-Demarara windows are combined with half-shutters.

GRENADA

Government House, in St. George's, was built in 1807 and extensively remodeled in 1887, when a two-story gallery was added. This addition has a Renaissance flavor on the lower level, with a simple arcade on the upper level.

Fig. 171. Government House, St. George's, Grenada, extensive remodeling of an 1807 building

TRINIDAD

Considerable French influence on Trinidadian architecture beginning in the late eighteenth century peaked in the late nineteenth in the designs of mansions for the cocoa and sugar plantations. Unfortunately, the French built their great houses of wood, and these have perished. Most of the existing mansions in Port of Spain were built about 1900 by wealthy merchants, using eclectic designs that show great exuberance. These houses defy style categories, but one thing is certain: they are not Georgian.

Roomor, the Roodal residence, is probably the most ornate and eclectic of the mansions that line the west side of Queen's Park Savannah. Designed by a French architect, it employs a multitude of shapes. Above the high ground floor runs a continuous balcony with an ornate cast-iron railing. A projecting canopy, without columns, protects the entrance. There is complete pandemonium on the roof, with an explosion of towers, domes, pediments, dormers, and cresting.

In the two-story Archbishop's Residence, designed in Ireland by an Irish architect and constructed from Irish marble and granite in 1904, arcades consume the walls on both floors. A square tower with an octagonal turret at one corner dominates the scheme. Complicated crenellations and machicolations provide a medieval flavor.

Whitehall was built of white coral limestone from Barbados by the owner of a large cocoa estate in 1903. Its basic shape is a rectangle, with occasional slight projections and strong horizontal accents. A balustrade conceals the roof. From the basement a double exterior stair leads up to the main level; there are two more floors. Engaged columns accent the front elevation, and many of the windows

Fig. 172. Roomor, Port of Spain, Trinidad, ornate and eclectic

Fig. 173. Corner detail of Roomor

Fig. 174. Archbishop's Residence, 1904, Port of Spain, Trinidad, an example of medieval eclecticism

Fig. 175. Whitehall, 1903, Port of Spain, Trinidad, an ornamented rectangular mass

have ornate trefoil-arch heads. Whitehall once housed the offices of the prime minister and now houses the Ministry of Environment and National Service.

Killarney, also known as Stolmeyer's Castle, 1904, was designed by a Scottish firm (see plate 17). The design employs a number of elements from Balmoral Castle in Scotland, such as the tower and the pepperpot turret that is corbeled from its wall. The diagonal wing projecting from the corner has a steep roof with a crowstep gable. A combination of pale yellow brick and blue-gray dressed stone, the building is now owned by the government of Trinidad and Tobago.

BAHAMAS

The large residences in the Bahamas were typically built of local quarried coral stone covered with stucco. In urban areas, the houses were usually two or three stories high, with louvered verandas placed appropriately to provide privacy, ventilation, and protection from the sun. Windows frequently had shutters, sometimes hinged from the top, sometimes from either side. The roofs were usually covered with cedar shingles, and dormer windows were common. The main level was often raised well above the ground to provide better air circulation and to lessen dampness. The kitchen with its hot fireplace was separate from the main house.

Greycliff, on West Hill Street in Nassau, about 1800, is Georgian in character but has many tropical characteristics such as wide verandas and latticework. Speculation suggests that a garrison may have been housed in the building at one time,

Fig. 176. Jacaranda, 1840s, Nassau, Bahamas, an example of Bahamian tropical

Fig. 177. Side and rear views of Jacaranda

because the cellars have low, thick walls and bars at the windows. In 1975, the house was converted into a small guest house and restaurant.

Jacaranda, a three-story residence on East Hill Street, Nassau, was built in the 1840s by Chief Justice Sir George Anderson. Louvered verandas completely cover the street (south) side, and occur on the two upper levels of the rear (north) elevation. The building has pink walls with white chamfered quoins, a string-course, watertable, and shingle roof. The site offers an excellent view of the harbor and ocean beyond. The Duke and Duchess of Windsor, who lived here, were responsible for major renovations.

The original walls of Cascadilla, on East Street, Nassau, about 1840, were of thick limestone. The building is located on densely landscaped property along with a number of ruins that may have been slave dwellings. The skillful construction of the main house suggests that it was probably built by ships' carpenters, and its careful design ensures good ventilation.

Buena Vista, on Delancy Street, Nassau, was probably built by John Murray, Earl of Dunmore, about 1790. It has experienced a number of additions, but the original hip-roof basic rectangle is Georgian, with pilasters. The building now houses a hotel and restaurant.

The style of Villa Doyle is unique in Nassau. The horizontal emphasis and the overhanging bracketed roof give it a Prairie style quality. Generous verandas occur outside the main structure, which is constructed of stone with quoins. A small projecting one-story bay window on the south has curious crenellations on its parapet. The builder of this elegant residence was a Bahamian, Sir William Doyle.

Fig. 178. Cascadilla, ca. 1840, Nassau, Bahamas, showing tropical detailing

Fig. 179. Buena Vista, ca. 1790, Nassau, Bahamas, Georgian with additions

Fig. 180. Villa Doyle, Nassau, Bahamas, Prairie style in the West Indies

PUERTO RICO

Few rural great houses were built in the Spanish islands, for many landlords lived in Spain, and most who lived in the Caribbean preferred to be in town. Management of the estates was typically left to administrators, whose dwellings have not survived. The very early townhouses of the planters were built of primitive masonry, with thick walls. In congested urban areas, rooms were usually oriented inward to a patio.

The family of Ponce de León had been living in the village of Caparra, but in 1521, the year of his death, they moved to San Juan and erected a wood house, which burned. The masonry construction of their next home, Casa Blanca, was

Fig. 181. Casa Blanca, 1527, San Juan, Puerto Rico, home of Ponce de León's descendants for 250 years

Fig. 182. La Fortaleza, San Juan, Puerto Rico, begun in 1540 as a fortress, later the governor's residence

begun in 1523 and finished in 1527. It was built to serve as a place of defense as well as a family home, and in 1529 attacking Caribs were repulsed with cannon fire from Casa Blanca. The building was occupied by Ponce de León's descendants for 250 years, at which time the Spanish government bought it to house its military commanders. During the twentieth century, it served as the residence of the U.S. Army commander in Puerto Rico until 1966. Since then, it has been a museum of sixteenth- and seventeenth-century Puerto Rican family life. Because plenty of land was available, Casa Blanca does not have the compactness of the typical Spanish urban house. Its white walls are relatively plain, with stringcourses at the roofline and parapets above. On one wing the parapet is crenelated, and a small tile roof shades the balcony. A few of the exterior doors and windows have small protective masonry hoods, and one prominent window is covered with a wood *reja*.

Construction of La Fortaleza, in San Juan, began in 1540 and consisted of a single circular tower at the corner of a quadrangle. It failed to serve well as a fortress and shortly became, instead, the official residence of the island's governors. Its major remodeling occurred in 1846 when, at the direction of Queen Isabella II, it was enlarged and given a palatial appearance. The oldest executive mansion still in use as such in the Western hemisphere, it has the original marble floors and mahogany stairway.

The town of Ponce flourished as a center of sugar, rum, and shipping from the late 1890s through the 1930s, and wealthy planters and successful merchants there hired the best available architects to design their elegant mansions. The Armstrong-Poventud Mansion was designed by Manuel Victor Domenech and built in 1901. A two-story, classical-revival building facing Plaza las Delicias, distinctive caryatids flank its entrance. Ionic pilasters define the building's three bays, and an ornate entablature occurs at the roofline, above which is a parapet. All openings have arch heads.

Serrallés Castle, 1926, designed by Pedro Adolfo de Castro, was the home of one of Ponce's richest families, who had accumulated their wealth from manufacturing Don Q Rum. This rambling, multilevel Spanish revival mansion sits on El Vigía Hill overlooking the city. Built around an open courtyard with fountains

Fig. 183. Armstrong-Poventud Mansion, 1901, Ponce, Puerto Rico, an example of classical revival

Fig. 184. Serrallés Castle, 1926, Ponce, Puerto Rico, rambling Spanish revival

and beautiful landscaping, the building is now a museum of Puerto Rican rum and sugarcane production.

CUBA

Many distinctive large residences grace the inner precincts of Havana, and master builders from Barcelona were responsible for much of the charm of this area. The ground-floor rooms of the typical Old Havana mansion were generally devoted to business, commerce, and storage; slaves or servants occupied a low-ceilinged half-floor above the storage areas. On the high-ceilinged levels where the family lived, louvered doors stretched from the floor to stained-glass transoms at the ceiling. Handsome balconies faced the street, and arcades surrounded inner courtyards. Rich materials adorned the interior surfaces.

Havana Cathedral Square is the site of a number of outstanding large residences. The Lombillo Mansion, 1587, included a tile kiln. Its first occupants, the Pedrosa family, lived there for over a hundred years. The Lombillos, the next residents, were there until the end of the nineteenth century. The building was opened in 1987 after two years of restoration as the Education Museum. The Mansion of the Marqués de Arcos, with a ground-floor arcade and three outstanding stained-glass panels above, was built in the early eighteenth century. The Mansion of the Marquéses de Aguas Claras is now a restaurant whose central dining patio and terrace overlook the square. The Palace of the Count de Bayona is now the Museum of Colonial Art. The building is renowned for its secular stained glass.

Charity House is a seventeenth-century building whose rococo entrance displays the Spanish coat of arms. It received its name from its owner's habit of providing dowries for young women who wished to marry but had no dowry.

Fig. 185. Lombillo Mansion, 1587, Havana, Cuba, now the Education Museum

Fig. 186. Mansion of the Marqués de Arcos, early eighteenth century, Havana, Cuba, colonial classicism

Fig. 187. Mansion of the Marquéses de Aguas Claras, Havana, Cuba, two stories around a central patio

Fig. 188. Patio, mansion of the Marquéses de Aguas Claras

Fig. 189. Palace of the Count de Bayona, Havana, showing magnificent stained glass

Fig. 190. Charity House, seventeenth century, Havana, Cuba, rococo entrance

Fig. 191. Patio, Charity House

Fig. 192. Doorway to patio, Charity House

Built around a spacious patio, it has magnificent interior Mudéjar doorways. The building is now used to display items related to children's activities.

The Palace of the Count of Santovenia is an early nineteenth-century building that serves as the enclosure for the eastern side of Arms Square. After the count's death in 1865, it was turned into a hotel and has since served a variety of functions.

Aldama Palace, built in 1840 on Fraternity Park, resembles an Italian palazzo and is considered one of Havana's most impressive nineteenth-century mansions. In the 1868 War of Independence, Spanish Volunteers sacked the palace, and the patriot owner was forced to flee the country. The luxurious salons were used as offices and storerooms for many years, and the building is now headquarters for the Institute of the History of the Communist Movement and the Socialist Revolution.

The enormous Presidential Palace, 1915, is constructed around two large open areas; one is topped with a glass-tiled dome, and the other is an open courtyard. The site of the 1957 unsuccessful attempt to assassinate President Fulgencio Batista, the building later became the Museum of the Revolution.

Xanadu was the 1920s winter mansion of Irénée DuPont in Varadero Beach. Its interior walls, inlaid ceilings, and staircases were made of precious Cuban woods: mahogany, ebony, and cedar. The floors were surfaced with Carrara marble. The top floor was a roofed ballroom, and each of its nine bedrooms had a private bath. The mansion has been converted to a restaurant.

Fig. 193. Palace of the Count of Santovenia, early nineteenth century, Havana, Cuba, the eastern enclosure to Arms Square

Fig. 194. Aldama Palace, 1840, Havana, Cuba, an Italian palazzo

Fig. 195. Colonnade, Aldama Palace

Fig. 196. Presidential Palace, 1915, Havana, Cuba, became the Museum of the Revolution

Plate 1. Old lighthouse, Port of
Spain, Trinidad

Plate 2. Colonial City Wall, San Juan, Puerto Rico

Plate 3. Ceramic tile painting of Old Square, Havana, Cuba

Plate 4. Public transportation "Tap-tap," Port-au-Prince, Haiti

Plate 5. Open market off Avenue John Brown Lalue, Port-au-Prince, Haiti, shows Caribbean energy

Plate 6. Ruins, Whim Plantation, St. Croix, U.S. Virgin Islands

Plate 7. Small residences, St. George's, Grenada

Plate 8. Bohios in rural Cuba

Plate 9. Residence frame, rural Haiti

Plate 10. Small urban residences, Pointe-au-Pitre, Guadeloupe

Plate 11. Row houses, Willemstad, Curaçao

Plate 12. Georgian House Restaurant, Basseterre, St. Kitts, eighteenth century, originally a residence

Plate 13. Villa Franca, suburban residence in Hastings, Barbados

Plate 14. Heavily ornamented Boissiere House, 1904, Port of Spain, Trinidad

Plate 15. The Deanery, ca. 1710, Nassau, probably the oldest residence in the Bahamas

Plate 16. Font-Ubides Mansion, 1912, with typical elegant details of early-twentieth-century Ponce, Puerto Rico

Plate 17. Killarney (Stolmeyer's Castle), 1904, Scottish medieval, after Balmoral

Plate 18. Alcazar, palace of Diego Columbus, 1510, Santo Domingo, Dominican Republic

Plate 19. Entrance steps, Sans Souci, the baroque palace of Henri Christophe, Milot, Haiti

Plate 20. Brievengat Estate veranda, Curaçao, early 1700s

Plate 21. Penha, 1708, the home and warehouse of a wealthy Dutch merchant, Punda section of Willemstad, Curaçao

Plate 22. Fort George, late 1600s, Brimstone Hill, St. Kitts

Plate 23. English Harbour, Antigua, the best hideaway for the British navy

Plate 24. Morne Fortuné barracks arcade, Castries, St. Lucia

Plate 25. Fort George, St. George's, Grenada

Plate 26. El Morro, begun 1589,
Havana, Cuba

Plate 27. Ozama Fortress, Santo Domingo, Dominican Republic, one of the oldest stone military structures in the New World

Plate 28. Fort Christian, 1680, center of the earliest Danish settlement, St. Thomas, U.S. Virgin Islands

Plate 29. Fort Frederik, 1760, Frederiksted, St. Croix, U.S. Virgin Islands

Plate 30. Rodney Memorial, 1790, Spanish Town, Jamaica, to commemorate the British victory at the Battle of the Saints

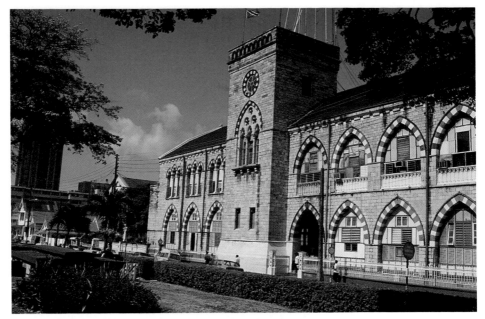

Plate 35. Police Headquarters, 1876, Port of Spain, Trinidad, polychrome Italian Gothic revival

Plate 36. Royal Victoria Institute, 1892, Port of Spain, Trinidad, now the National Museum

Plate 37. Nassau Public Library, 1799, Bahamas, originally used as a jail

Plate 38. Palace of the Captains General, 1792, one of the earliest buildings in Havana, Cuba

Plate 39. Old Capitol, 1929, Havana, Cuba, patterned after the capitol in Washington, D.C.

Plate 40. National Palace, 1918, Port-au-Prince, Haiti; two predecessors were destroyed by revolutions

Plate 41. Schoelcher Library, Fort-de-France, Martinique, earlier an exhibit building at the 1899 World Exposition in Paris

Plate 42. Courthouse, 1825, Philipsburg, Sint Maarten, an unpretentious building

Plate 43. Cathedral of the Diocese of Jamaica, 1699, Spanish Town, the oldest Anglican cathedral outside Great Britain

Plate 44. Holy Trinity Roman Catholic Cathedral, 1911, Kingston, Jamaica, in Byzantine-revival style

Plate 45. St. George's Parish Church, 1859, Basseterre, St. Kitts, in Romanesque and Gothic styles

Plate 46. Cathedral of St. John the Divine, 1848, dominates the town of St. John's, Antigua

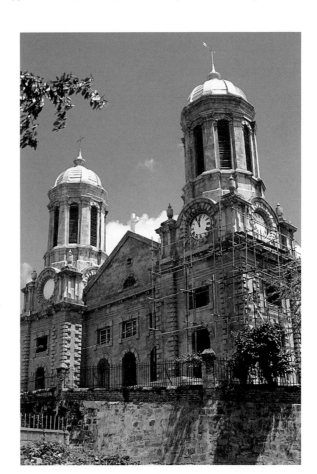

Plate 47. Cathedral of the Immaculate Conception, 1895, Castries, St. Lucia, one of the largest church floor areas in the Caribbean

Plate 48. Interior, Cathedral of the Immaculate Conception, 1895, Castries, St. Lucia

Plate 49. Interior, hammerbeam trusses, St. Patricks Roman Catholic Cathedral, 1898, Bridgetown, Barbados

Plate 50. Roman Catholic Cathedral of the Immaculate Conception, 1832, Port of Spain, Trinidad, with twin octagonal Gothic towers

Plate 51. Jinnah Memorial Mosque, St. Joseph, Trinidad, serves a large East Indian population

Plate 52. San Juan Cathedral, 1540, Puerto Rico, Italian baroque influence

Plate 53. Cathedral of Havana, ca. 1777, Cuba, heavily sculptured baroque

Plate 54. Side aisle vault, Cathedral of
Santa Maria la Menor, 1541, Santo
Domingo, Dominican Republic

Plate 55. Notre Dame Cathedral, early 1900s, Port-au-Prince, Haiti, cast-concrete Romanesque

Plate 56. Interior frescoes, Holy Trinity Episcopal Cathedral, 1929, Port-au-Prince, Haiti

Plate 57. St. Louis Cathedral, 1895, Fort-de-France, Martinique, cast-iron design by Gustave Eiffel

Plate 58. Church of St. Peter and St. Paul, Pointe-au-Pitre, Guadeloupe, Italian baroque exterior

Plate 59. Mikve Israel-Emanuel Synagogue, 1733, Willemstad, Curaçao, the oldest synagogue in continuous use in the Western hemisphere

Plate 60. Queen's Royal College, 1904, Port of Spain, Trinidad, showing multiple use of materials and colors

Plate 61. García Lorca, 1837, the Great Theater of Havana, Cuba

Plate 62. Puerto Rico's 1883 Exposition-Fair, Ponce; its main building was to become the home of Ponce's Fireman's Corps

Plate 63. San Miguel Baños Hotel, 1926, San Miguel, Cuba, once the fashionable place to "take the waters"

Plate 64. Art nouveau window, Banco Santander, 1924, Ponce, Puerto Rico

DOMINICAN REPUBLIC

Casa del Cordón gets its name from the large carved rope around the doorway, which represents the Order of St. Francis. Built in 1502 by an explorer who had accompanied Columbus on his first voyage, the house was one of the first in Santo Domingo to be built completely of stone. Diego Columbus, son of Christopher, later lived here with his wife, Marie de Toledo, and it is said that two of their children were born here.

Nicholás de Ovando, first colonial governor and founder of Santo Domingo, built his palace on the Ozama River about 1510. The restored palace forms the nucleus for an elegant small hotel.

Also in the sixteenth century, three houses with connecting facades were built on Calle las Mercedes in Santo Domingo: the House of the Jesuits, the House of the Gargoyles, and the Don Juan de Villoria House. Only the center house, with its gargoyles and small iron balconies, displays ornaments on the street facade. (It is believed that these gargoyles once adorned the cathedral.) In typical fashion, these three houses were primarily oriented to inner courtyards, with minimum window openings to the street.

The palace of Diego Columbus, called the Alcazar, was considered one of the most impressive residences in the New World, reportedly built by 1,000 Indian laborers working under the supervision of twenty-eight Spanish master builders for several years, completing construction in 1510 (see plate 18). Diego followed Nicholás de Ovando as governor of the colony. He located his palace so as to

Fig. 197. Casa del Cordón, 1502, Santo Domingo, Dominican Republic, one of the first all-stone houses in the city

Fig. 198. Casa Nicholás de Ovando, original portion ca. 1510, Santo Domingo, Dominican Republic, now an elegant small hotel

Fig. 199. Casa Nicholás de
Ovando interior

Fig. 200. Three houses on Calle las Mercedes, sixteenth century,
Santo Domingo, Dominican Republic

Fig. 201. Entrance to the Alcazar, palace of Diego
Columbus, 1510, Santo Domingo, Dominican
Republic

Fig. 202. The Captains' Palace, 1509, Santo
Domingo, Dominican Republic, with many rooms
relating to interior courtyards

overlook the river to the east and the Plaza de Armas to the west, and it became
the headquarters of the Spanish court in America. It is severely rectangular, with
two-story arcaded loggie on the east and west elevations. The stonework is excellent, and no nails were used in the wood-roof construction. In the arcade, segmental arches are supported on round columns, and Mudéjar details embellish
the stonework at the entrance.

Fig. 203. Porcelain Museum, once the
Vicini residence, ca. 1900, Santo
Domingo, Dominican Republic, inspired
by the Alhambra Palace

The Captains' Palace, 1502–9, is actually a complex of several palaces. Its
many rooms relate to interior courtyards, and the windowless exterior is unadorned except for the entrance details. The building is now the Museum of the
Royal Houses, with displays covering the period from the sixteenth century to
the proclamation of independence from Spain in 1821.

At the turn of the century, the Vicini family built a residence in Santo
Domingo inspired by the Alhambra Palace. It has been home to a number of the
country's most prominent figures and is now the Porcelain Museum.

HAITI

The most spectacular residence built in Haiti was Sans Souci, a baroque palace
located near the village of Milot on the north coast (see plate 19). Called the
"Versailles of the New World," it was built by Henri Christophe starting in 1804,
when Haiti had gained independence from France. French architects were employed in the construction of this enormous building, which had four levels and
covered a land area of approximately 14,000 square feet. Built of stuccoed stone
and brick, it enclosed spacious halls, dramatic staircases, and elaborate suites for
the ruler and his large retinue. There was even a private theater, and the finest
woods, marble, mosaics, and mirrors available were used in the interior, often
imported from Europe. Under the floors, conduits carried cold water to cool the

Fig. 204. Sans Souci, begun 1804, Milot, Haiti, the baroque palace home of Henri Christophe

Fig. 205. French Renaissance influence, Port-au-Prince, Haiti

rooms. In 1811, Christophe became King Henri, and his increasingly despotic reign eventually led to revolution. As the rebelling troops approached Milot, Christophe was confined by illness at Sans Souci and realized that he could not escape. Rather than be captured, he shot himself with a pistol in his bedroom. In 1842, an earthquake badly damaged the palace, but even in ruins it remains an imposing edifice.

Fig. 206. Roman Catholic Bishop's Residence, Port-au-Prince, Haiti, classical symmetry within a tropical scheme

As has been mentioned, much of Haiti's eighteenth-century architecture was destroyed in the fight for independence. In the turn-of-the-century residential architecture in Port-au-Prince, the influence of the French Renaissance is evident in such details as dormered mansard roofs fronted by balustrades, openings with segmental-arch heads, and walls with pilasters. The design of these examples seldom takes into account the climatic demands of their tropical location, except that window openings are large, sometimes extending to the floor.

Some examples nevertheless manage to retain their formality while including architectural characteristics that promote comfort in a tropical climate. The Roman Catholic Bishop's Residence, across from the Cathedral, is one of these. It is classically symmetrical, with balustrades on each of the three levels and a projecting central pavilion. All of this is accomplished within a tropical scheme, however, with high ceilings and open galleries that wrap entirely around the building.

Other Haitian residences accomplish these qualities with more vernacular materials and design, using wood siding on the main structure, while the spacious galleries reflect varied designs in their fretwork and railings. Full-height pairs of doors may have louvered shutters swinging into the rooms and solid shutters opening onto the galleries.

The most fascinating residential examples are, of course, those that pay homage to no historical precedent, which occur most exuberantly in the roof forms with their steep-pitched, steeplelike projections with pinnacles. These are

Fig. 207. Tropical wood vernacular, Port-au-Prince, Haiti

Fig. 208. Residential Haitian exuberance, Port-au-Prince, Haiti

usually supported by galleries or balconies decorated with great abandon at the fascias and railings. The main structure to which these are attached is frequently half-timber with brick infill.

MARTINIQUE

Le Gaoulé, about 1740, is probably the oldest residence on Martinique. With its hipped tile roof and dormers, it is reminiscent of eighteenth-century country houses in France. It is built of rubble stone, with segmental arches spanning its door and window openings. Residential French colonial design at this time had

Fig. 209. Cast-iron gallery on a residence, Fort-de-France, Martinique, that now houses the director of sanitation

only partially responded to the climatic demands of the tropics: there is a veranda on only one face of the house.

Cast iron is used in the structures of some of the later large homes in Fort-de-France. The former residence that now houses the director of sanitation has a cast-iron, two-story gallery attached to wood-frame construction. The traditional two-foot masonry base also occurs on this building.

GUADELOUPE

The Municipal Museum, Pointe-au-Pitre, is a converted residence and another excellent example of cast-iron architecture, which here establishes a strict module for the building. Except for the three entrance bays, the design of the building proper is extremely restrained. By contrast, the sheet-metal fascias and the cast-iron railings add frivolity to the composition. Simple louvered shutters occur at all openings. An insignificant third floor protrudes slightly above the upper gallery.

CURAÇAO

Among the most impressive buildings in Curaçao are the Dutch plantation mansions, called *landhuizen* (land houses), which date from the seventeenth and eighteenth centuries. Most have been deserted or destroyed; fortunately, a few remain. One of the most outstanding is Brievengat, an estate of 1,275 acres northeast of Willemstad. The date of construction is uncertain but is probably in

Fig. 210. Residence with excellent cast-iron architecture, converted to Municipal Museum, Pointe-au-Pitre, Guadeloupe

Fig. 211. Brievengat Estate, Curaçao, early 1700s, an impressive plantation mansion

Fig. 212. Brievengat gable

Fig. 213. Merchant's home, 1750, Otrobanda section of Willemstad, Curaçao, now the Otrobanda Police
Station

the early 1700s. Hurricane damage and neglect took their toll on this mansion,
but in 1954 the Society for the Preservation of Monuments carefully restored it
to its original condition. Raised above a sloping site, the house is fronted with a
generous terrace and surrounded by a retaining wall with towers at the corners.
Originally watchtowers, they were later used to imprison slaves, and it is popu-
larly believed that they were also the scenes of extramarital rendezvous. An arcaded veranda spans the front of the house, and curvilinear gables terminate the
red tile roof, which is punctuated with ornate dormers (see plate 20). The
kitchen has been meticulously restored, and appropriate antiques furnish the
other rooms.

Fig. 214. Merchant's home roof features

In the Punda section of Willemstad, the original buildings were owned by wealthy merchants, combining street-level warehouse space with upper-level residences. Because Punda was enclosed by a wall, space eventually was at a premium. The oldest and probably the best known of these buildings is Penha, 1708, which faces onto three streets (see plate 21). Well maintained, it has beautiful curvilinear gables, columns, and arcades, with elaborate stucco ornaments picked out in yellow and white.

The development of the Otrobanda section of Willemstad began when Punda ran out of space, with its first fourteen lots laid out in 1707. Because there was no walled enclosure around this section, larger lots allowed more spacious houses to be built. On Molenplein is a large and beautifully restored merchant's home that dates from 1750. The most important floor is elevated, accessed by an exterior double staircase. Interestingly, the end gables of the main body of the house are of different designs. A chimney indicates the location of the kitchen wing. The mansion now houses the Otrobanda Police Station.

U.S. VIRGIN ISLANDS

The great house on Whim Plantation, near Frederiksted, was spared when many others were torched during a slave uprising on St. Croix because its owner was a French woman who had brought her own servants with her, and they remained loyal. Constructed of well-laid stone in the late 1700s, the house is distinctive in plan because of its curved north end. Its simple design includes semicircular tympana above its entrances and triangular pediments over the windows. All the openings are shuttered. The late eighteenth-century Dane's idea of a proper

Fig. 215. Whim Plantation great house, St. Croix, U.S. Virgin Islands, the late eighteenth-century Dane's idea of a proper country mansion

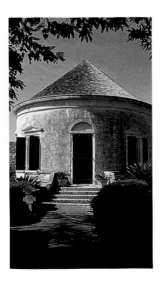

Fig. 216. Entrance, Whim Plantation great house

country mansion, Whim has been beautifully restored by the St. Croix Landmarks Society.

The Baron von Bretton House, in Charlotte Amalie, St. Thomas, was built in 1818 by an affluent merchant and landowner. An interior courtyard was surrounded by an arched and columned gallery, with shops and storage on the ground floor and living quarters on the upper two floors. Flat roofs doubled as terraces outside some of the rooms. The building is now the Enid M. Baa Public Library.

Located next to the Lutheran church on Norre Gade in Charlotte Amalie, Bethania was built in 1827 to replace an eighteenth-century residence destroyed by the 1826 fire that razed most of the buildings on Government Hill. The building employs a minimum of decorations but achieves a sculptural quality with its good proportions and simplicity.

Cathrineberg was a plantation on the outskirts of Charlotte Amalie. The neo-

Fig. 217. Baron von Bretton House, 1818, Charlotte Amalie, St. Thomas, U.S. Virgin Islands, mixed occupancy

Fig. 218. Bethania, 1827, Charlotte Amalie, St. Thomas, U.S.V.I., simple design with good proportions

classical great house was built in 1830, high above town on Denmark Hill, raised on a basement platform that once contained storage, services, and a stable. A monumental stair leads to the entrance veranda at the upper level. The parapet above the roof is paneled and supports unusual acroteria at the corners. When it was no longer a plantation house, it became the residence of the director of the Danish West India Company and is now the Danish Consulate.

Fig. 219. Cathrineberg, 1830, Denmark Hill, St. Thomas, U.S.V.I., a neoclassical great house

Fig. 220. Frederiksberg, 1820s, outskirts of Charlotte Amalie, St. Thomas, U.S.V.I., another classical villa

Another country villa on the opposite outskirts of Charlotte Amalie is Frederiksberg, built in the 1820s by a St. Thomas merchant. It, too, is classical-revival style, with a columned portico and formal staircase facing the harbor. The building has been incorporated into the complex of Bluebeard's Castle Hotel and an unfortunate remodeling has occurred on the pediment of the entrance portico.

Fig. 221. Frederik Lutheran Parsonage, ca. 1725, Charlotte Amalie, St. Thomas, U.S.V.I., a simple three-story, seven-bay building

Frederik Lutheran Parsonage, on Government Hill in Charlotte Amalie, about 1725, is an extremely simple three-story, seven-bay building. The lowest level is solid masonry, stuccoed, with a single, slightly off-center arched opening. Open verandas occur on the two upper levels, supported by square masonry columns on the middle level and square iron columns on the uppermost. Shuttered doors open onto the verandas.

CHAPTER 7

MILITARY FACILITIES

The great competition for the Caribbean islands among European powers resulted in intense military activity in the area. A military presence was also needed to protect the citizenry against the countless bands of pirates and buccaneers who pillaged ships and raided coastal towns, and attack by Carib Indians was always a danger in the days of early settlement. It is not surprising, therefore, that much of the earliest Caribbean architecture concerned itself with these dangers. The massive nature of the resulting walls and fortifications ensured that many examples would endure. Others have disappeared as a result of neglect, disinterest, and the need for urban expansion.

JAMAICA

When the English took Jamaica in 1655, they realized the strategic importance of Port Royal on the south coast and almost immediately began building Fort Cromwell, which became Fort Charles when Charles II came to the British throne. Five more forts were added in this vicinity: Fort Walker, Fort James, Fort Carlisle, Sea Fort (later called Fort Rupert), and Morgan's Line.

Fig. 222. Fort Charles, Port Royal, Jamaica, a critical defense location in the seventeenth and eighteenth centuries

In the seventeenth and eighteenth centuries the English, unlike the French, kept many of their naval vessels in the Caribbean year-round, and the defenses at Port Royal were critical to the safety of their ships in Jamaica.

The functioning of these facilities was disrupted on 7 June 1692, when three earthquake shocks within two minutes sent the better part of Port Royal beneath the sea. Of the six forts there, only Morgan's Line and Fort Charles were left more or less intact, the latter having sunk some three and one-half feet during the disturbance.

Fort Charles was built of brick. Its thick surrounding walls had battlemented parapets and arched openings where cannons were positioned. Horatio Nelson briefly commanded the fort when he was in his twenties, and the fort's elevated walkway is still referred to as Nelson's Quarterdeck. His offices and living quarters have been converted into the Maritime Museum.

A unique military building in Port Royal is the Old Naval Hospital, built in 1819 to replace the hospital that burned in 1815. The frame of the new two-story structure was made of prefabricated cast-iron units imported from Bradford, England. These units were placed on a raft foundation, with all columns linked to this foundation beneath the massive structure. The actual building enclosure was constructed of stone; open colonnades ran around it at both levels. The soundness of the Old Naval Hospital has allowed it to survive numerous hurricanes, as well as the earthquake of 1907. When Hurricane Charlie destroyed many residences and other buildings in Port Royal in 1951, the Old Naval Hospital suffered only minor damage. In fact, many Port Royal people took shelter from the storm in the hospital building, and some lived there for as long as eight years.

Fig. 223. Old print of 1692 earthquake, Port Royal, Jamaica

Fig. 224. Horatio Nelson's quarters, Fort Charles, Port Royal, Jamaica

Fig. 225. Old Naval Hospital, 1819, Port Royal, Jamaica

About 1800 along England's coasts, a number of defensive round Martello towers were built with provision for firing guns from the roof. A few were also constructed in the Caribbean, and one that was part of the defense network around Kingston Harbour still exists at Harbour View. An interior spiral stair leads to the top of the tower, which is an example of excellent stone masonry.

Among the many other forts built in Jamaica are the ruins of Fort George, constructed in 1733 in Port Antonio with positions for twenty-two cannons. A

Fig. 226. Martello Tower, Harbour View, Jamaica

1675 description states that Morant Bay had a platform with three guns, and a later drawing shows nine gun positions there. The sturdy stone barracks of Fort Balcarres, built in 1811 to defend Falmouth Harbour on the north coast, now house the Falmouth All Age School.

ST. KITTS

Fort George, on Brimstone Hill, was under construction for 100 years beginning in the late 1600s and has been called "the Gibraltar of the West Indies" (see plate 22). At an elevation of 750 feet above the Caribbean, its defenses consisted of five bastions spread out over thirty acres. It was considered impregnable by the British, for enemy troops would have to ascend the steep slope and overcome the various bastions while under fire from the heavy guns above. In 1782, however, the French accomplished this feat, although they were driven out by the British the following year. The extraordinary structures on Brimstone Hill are considered to rival many European examples in their design and execution. This area is now a national park.

ANTIGUA

Antigua, another location where the British fleet was kept year-round, although heavily fortified, saw little service, for the island lay to the windward and was difficult for sailing ships to reach.

Fort James was built on the promontory at the north entrance to St. John's Harbour. The original fortifications date from about 1675, although most of the existing structures were built in 1749. At its largest, the fort boasted thirty-six guns and accommodations for seventy men.

Fig. 227. Fort George, late 1600s, Brimstone Hill, St. Kitts, "the Gibraltar of the West Indies"

Fig. 228. Fort James, Antigua, protected St. John's north harbor entrance

English Harbour offered a perfect hideaway for the British navy, and here Horatio Nelson labored to prepare his fleet for the eventual victory over Napoleon at Trafalgar (see plate 23). The ship maintenance area established in 1725 is now referred to as Nelson's Dockyard, although the admiral was not responsible for its development and his writings make frequent reference to his dislike of the place. The dockyard is now a national park, and considerable restoration has adapted the various buildings to new usage as shops, inns, and restaurants.

High above Nelson's Dockyard is Shirley Heights, a fortification started in 1781. These were difficult times for the British, who had just lost the American colonies and several of their Caribbean islands, retaining only Antigua, Barbados,

Fig. 229. Nelson's Dockyard, English Harbour, Antigua, now a national park

Fig. 230. Shirley Heights restored building, Antigua

Fig. 231. Shirley Heights barracks ruins

and Jamaica. With the establishment of peace in 1815 after the Battle of Waterloo, the facilities at English Harbour and Shirley Heights became less important, and by 1899 the Royal Navy had left. Considerable deterioration had occurred by the 1950s when restoration began, but these locations are now major tourist attractions.

ST. LUCIA

St. Lucia was one of the most extreme examples of British-French rivalry; the island changed hands fourteen times between the two before it became British in 1814. There are many architectural reminders of this era on the 800-foot-high Morne Fortuné, where the nation currently in power often added to previous military building by the rival power. In the nineteenth century, the British embarked on a building program that was to provide barracks for 20,000 men (see plate 24). Many of these yellow-brick barracks were constructed in the 1890s, just a few years before orders came from London to abandon all building and evacuate the garrison. These buildings have now been restored and adapted for use as residential apartments, a secondary school, a teachers' training college, and a branch campus of the University of the West Indies. Similarly, the restored barracks on the slopes of Vigie Point have been adapted for use as office space.

Fig. 232. Morne Fortuné barracks

Fig. 233. Picture postcard of the regiment, 1899, Vigie Point, St. Lucia

Fig. 234. Adaptive use of Vigie Point barracks, St. Lucia, as office space

BARBADOS

Because Barbados was not sought after by the various European powers, sea defenses were minimal, consisting mostly of small forts and batteries. The location was important, however, as another of the three Caribbean locations where British sailing vessels were kept year-round. The island also became the main headquarters of the British forces in the Lesser Antilles, which led to the construction of St. Ann's Fort beginning in 1704.

Although the British garrison withdrew from Barbados in 1905, many of the arcaded barracks buildings required to house the 4,000 soldiers remain. The gar-

Fig. 235. Garrison prison, Bridgetown, ca. 1820, now the Barbados Museum

Fig. 236. Garrison hospital, ca. 1806, Bridgetown, Barbados, now converted to apartments

Fig. 237. St. Ann's Fort Guard House, completed 1824, Bridgetown, Barbados, until recently a private club

rison prison, about 1820, is now the Barbados Museum. The garrison hospital, about 1806, has been converted to apartments. The Savannah, once a parade ground, is now a racetrack. St. Ann's Fort Guard House, with its early Victorian-style tower, was, until recently, the Savannah Club, a private club. The Barbados Defence Force occupies several of the other buildings. Charles Fort, of which little remains, is on the grounds of the government-owned Hilton Hotel.

GRENADA

Grenada is another island that shuttled back and forth between the British and the French, prompting six forts to be built on the high points of St. George's, the capital.

In 1706, the French built Fort Royale on the end of the peninsula (see plate 25). When the British took over, they renamed it Fort George. The existing military barracks at that location are from the French era and now house the Grenada Police Headquarters and Police Training School; cadets drill in the courtyard.

Another barracks building, built by the French in the center of St. George's in 1704, now houses the National Museum. Four forts started by the French on Richmond Hill were completed by the British. The best preserved of these is Fort Frederick.

Fig. 238. Fort George Barracks, eighteenth century, St. George's, Grenada

Fig. 239. French Barracks, 1704, St. George's, Grenada, now the National Museum

Fig. 240. Fort Frederick, St. George's, Grenada

TRINIDAD

Fort George, at an elevation of 1,100 feet, was built in 1804 to guard Port of Spain. Its use as a signal station became obsolete with the invention of the wireless.

St. James Barracks, in Port of Spain, was built in 1827 according to designs sent out by the British War Office. An arcaded basement supports a colonnade

Fig. 241. St. James Barracks, 1827, Port of Spain, Trinidad, now a training school for police

above, and the central pavilion has a pseudopediment. The barracks became a training school for police in 1906.

Fort San Andres, guarding the Port of Spain Harbour, was built as a battery in 1787. In recent times, it became the headquarters of the Trinidad and Tobago Police Service Traffic Branch, before being designated the National Museum.

BAHAMAS

Fort Nassau, the first fort on New Providence Island, was built in 1695 when the Bahama Islands were under the proprietorship of the Carolina colony. It suffered early attacks from the French and Spanish. Rebuilt several times, it was demolished in 1837 to make room for military barracks, in turn torn down in 1899 to make way for the Hotel Colonial.

Fort Fincastle was built on Bennet's Hill in 1789 by Lord Dunmore. Its original firepower was two 24-pounders, two 32-pounders, and two 12-pounders, but none of these guns was ever used to defend Nassau. The fort was used as a lighthouse until 1816, when it became a signal tower.

Fort Charlotte, also completed in 1789 by Lord Dunmore, was named after the consort and wife of King George III. Its purpose was to guard the west entrance to Nassau's harbor. A dry moat was dug along its north side, the stone from its excavation used for the upper walls. The fort was constructed in three sections: the east portion was Fort Charlotte proper; the middle bastion was Fort Stanley; the west portion, Fort D'Arcy, was built later and housed the principal stores and powder magazine. A furnace located here was used to heat shot, fired

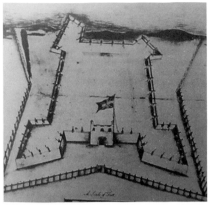

Fig. 242. Old Print of Fort Nassau, 1695, New Providence Island, Bahamas

Fig. 243. Old picture postcard, Fort Fincastle, 1789, Nassau, Bahamas

Fig. 244. Fort Charlotte, 1789, Nassau, Bahamas, a fort that was never active

red-hot at enemy ships to set the sails on fire. New Providence Island was never attacked after the building of Fort Charlotte.

PUERTO RICO

La Fortaleza, started in 1540, was originally a single circular defense tower built at one corner of a walled quadrangle. When its lack of military value was realized, it became the residence of the island's governors (see in "Large Residences" chapter).

San Felipe del Morro, commonly referred to as El Morro, begun in 1540, was named after King Philip III of Spain. *Morro* means "headland" or "promontory."

Fig. 245. El Morro, begun 1540, completed 1775, the most strategic fort protecting San Juan, Puerto Rico

Fig. 246. San Cristobal, begun 1640, built to protect San Juan, Puerto Rico, against land attack

Considered the most strategic of the various forts built to defend San Juan, El Morro was not completed until 1775. It was built on six levels, with thick walls as much as 140 feet high. Although the fort was intended primarily to prevent attack from the sea, its landward side was protected by a deep moat outside the wall, accessed by drawbridge. Inside, El Morro contained all the facilities of a living citadel: barracks, dungeons, armory, chapel, offices, and storage. The small fort of El Cañuelo across the bay, designed to provide crossfire with El Morro,

Fig. 247. San Jerónimo, 1788, the smallest and last fortification for San Juan, Puerto Rico

Fig. 248. La Princesa, 1837, San Juan, Puerto Rico, an artillery practice camp, for many years a jail, now offices of the Puerto Rican Tourism Company

was built in 1640 and reconstructed about 1660. El Morro withstood an attack by Sir Francis Drake in 1595 and was taken only once, in 1598, by the Earl of Cumberland, whose occupancy was terminated by an epidemic of dysentery.

San Cristobal, begun in 1640, was built to assist El Morro defend against land attack. Its five independent units rise 150 feet above the sea and cover twenty-seven acres. The central stronghold could be taken only after the five outer structures had been captured. The fort reached its full size in 1678 but was not finally completed until 1783.

San Jerónimo, built in 1788, was the smallest and last of the San Juan fortifi-

Fig. 249. El Arsenal, 1900, built by the Spanish to patrol the swamps around San Juan, Puerto Rico

Fig. 250. Santa Elena gunpowder magazine, San Juan, Puerto Rico, now an art studio

cations, rebuilt after being badly damaged by the British in 1797. It now lies in the grounds of the Caribe Hilton Hotel and houses a military museum.

La Princesa, built in 1837, was an artillery practice camp before becoming a jail. The original building was on one level, with a second story added about 1910. The small hospital addition was built in 1882. The building currently houses offices for the Tourism Company.

El Arsenal was built by the Spanish in 1800 as a base for 30 small boats that patrolled the mangrove swamps around San Juan. It now houses exhibit galleries used for rotating art exhibitions.

The Ballajá Barracks, built in 1850, was the largest nineteenth-century structure built by the Spanish in the New World. The Santa Elena gunpowder magazine, an interesting vaulted structure, is now used as studio space by the Fine Arts School.

CUBA

The first Cuban fortress was La Real Fuerza Castle, in Havana, begun in 1558. Surrounded by a moat with a drawbridge and facing seaward, for centuries this fortress guarded the portside entrance to Arms Square, the original center of Havana. It is now the Arms Museum.

Two other sixteenth-century fortresses are Los Tres Reyes del Morro Castle (El Morro), begun 1589, and San Salvador de la Punta, 1600, both designed by the Italian engineer Juan Bautista Antonelli. Facing each other across the entrance to the port, they could be connected by an iron chain above the water to prevent the entry of enemy ships (see plate 26). The lighthouse at El Morro was built in 1844. El Morro served as a jail from 1904 to 1974.

Immediately after the British left Cuba in 1763, the Spanish engineer Silvestre Abarca designed the more modern La Cabaña fortress, behind El Morro, which

Fig. 251. Old print of Havana Harbor, Cuba

Fig. 252. La Real Fuerza Castle, Havana, begun 1558, the first Cuban fortress

Fig. 253. San Salvador de la Punta, 1600, Havana, Cuba

Fig. 254. Cabana Fortress, 1774, Havana, Cuba

Fig. 255. Remnant of old city wall, Havana, Cuba

was completed in 1774. The traditional 9:00 P.M. cannon shot is still fired from its parapets every evening.

The successful invasion of Havana by the British proved the old city wall a dubious means of defense; in 1863, demolition began. Only fragments of the wall remain, including a small section and a guard post in front of the present railroad terminal.

DOMINICAN REPUBLIC

Santo Domingo, capital of the Dominican Republic, was located on the easily defensible corner of land where the Ozama River empties into the Caribbean Sea. On the land side of the settlement, a fortified wall extended from the river to the sea.

Ozama Fortress, located here, is one of the oldest stone military structures in the New World, called La Fuerza in colonial days (see plate 27). The Tower of Homage, its principal structure, was built in 1503. The military buildings around the tower, built in 1787, were later enlarged. The Powder House in this complex displays the coat of arms of Spain's King Charles III.

HAITI

The early French forts in Haiti were primarily coastal, located on the north side of the island. The English also built some forts, although they never had a secure foothold here. Following the revolution, Jean-Jacques Dessalines ordered the

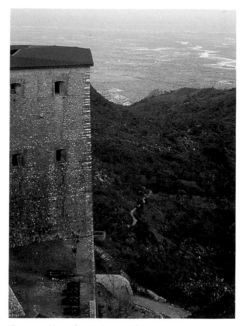

Fig. 256. The Citadel, begun 1804, elevation 3,000 feet, near Milot, Haiti

Fig. 257. View from the Citadel

Fig. 258. Dessalines Barracks, 1910, Port-au-Prince, Haiti

construction of forts all over the country as insurance against an attempt by the French to retake Haiti.

Work continued sporadically for fifteen years on the largest fort, begun in 1804 by Dessalines, but Henri Christophe was responsible for most of its construction. This largest mountain fortress in the New World, the Citadel, La Ferrière, dominates an area near the village of Milot on the north coast. Up a mountain trail, an army of conscripted former slaves dragged tons of masonry, 365 heavy bronze cannons, and a huge supply of cannonballs to install it more than 3,000 feet up, atop a peak. It is said that in the process 2,000 of the 10,000 laborers lost their lives.

The walls of the Citadel range from 80 to 140 feet high and up to 20 feet thick. Designed by a Haitian engineer, Henri Beese, and the Frenchman Henri Barre, the plan is an irregular quadrilateral shape, culminating at a point directed due north toward Milot. The fortress was intended to house 10,000 troops and had a royal apartment of more than forty rooms. In anticipation of lengthy sieges, there were cisterns for water, vast storerooms for food, and spacious magazines of powder and shot.

In the courtyard of the fortress, a small white tomb marks the grave of Henri Christophe, whose body was carried here from Sans Souci. The Citadel is being restored as a UNESCO world heritage site.

In Port-au-Prince, behind the National Palace, lie the extensive Dessalines Barracks designed by Georges Baussan in 1910. These two- and three-story masonry buildings show considerable French influence. Prominent dormers connected with balustrades occur in mansard roofs. Dentiled stringcourses define the floor levels.

MARTINIQUE

The French were the first settlers in Martinique, and they defended the island from the British. Fort Royale, later Fort St. Louis, was begun in the 1670s to guard the anchorage of Fort-de-France, the capital. Its system of fleches, moats, and ramparts was formidable, and it is still used as a military facility.

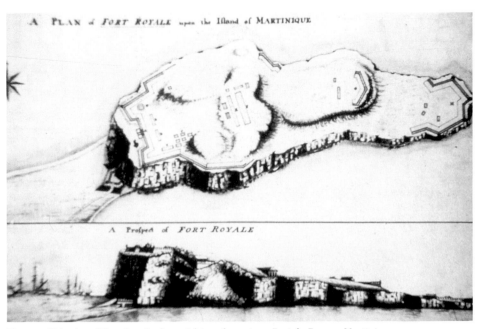

Fig. 259. Old print of Fort Royale, late eighteenth century, Fort-de-France, Martinique

Fig. 260. Fort St. Louis, Fort-de-France, Martinique

Fig. 261. Fort St. Louis, 1786, Marigot, St. Martin

Fig. 262. Fort Amsterdam, late seventeenth century, Philipsburg, Sint Maarten

ST. MARTIN/SINT MAARTEN

The French and Dutch were not always as neighborly as they are today. The island underwent sixteen changes of flag, claimed at various times by Spain, France, the Netherlands, and England. The ruins of Fort St. Louis overlook Marigot, the French capital. This hilltop fort was built by the French in 1786.

On a sliver of land at Philipsburg, capital of the Dutch portion of the island, lie the remains of Fort Amsterdam. This late-seventeenth-century fort built by the Dutch stands on the foundations of an earlier Spanish fort.

CURAÇAO

Waterfort, on the Punda side of Willemstad and at the level of St. Anna Bay, was begun in the sixteenth century and was the sole original defense of this area. Fort Amsterdam, behind it, was begun in 1634, and eventually took the form of a quadrilateral, with bastions at each corner.

Two forts at higher elevations were added to the defense effort. Fort Nassau was built in 1796 and improved in 1804. Fort Waakzaamheid, its contemporary, perched on a hill overlooking Otrobanda and was the object of a twenty-six-day siege by Captain William Bligh.

In 1827, Waterfort was considerably enlarged and improved and, in the following year across the bay, Riffort, a twin of Waterfort, was completed, with fifty-six cannons. The crossfire of these two forts made St. Anna Bay inaccessible for hostile vessels. With this assurance, Fort Amsterdam ceased to be critical, so it was redesigned to accommodate government offices and to serve as a residence for high-ranking government officials and officers.

In 1956, part of the Curaçao Plaza Hotel was built on top of Waterfort, and the east portion of the fort became a shopping mall. Adaptive uses have also occurred at the other forts: the dungeons of Riffort now house two restaurants and a bar, Fort Nassau boasts a restaurant and a discotheque, and Fort Waakzaamheid has a dining tavern.

Fig. 263. Waterfort, sixteenth century, Willemstad, Curaçao

Fig. 264. Fort Amsterdam, begun 1634, Willemstad, Curaçao

Fig. 265. Riffort, 1828, Otrobanda side of Willemstad, Curaçao

U.S. VIRGIN ISLANDS

In 1672, the Danes began constructing fortifications in the Danish West Indies. Fort Christian, named for King Christian V, was completed in 1680 and became the center of the settlement (see plate 28). It is the oldest standing structure on St. Thomas, a survivor of the fires and hurricanes that destroyed much of Charlotte Amalie in the eighteenth and nineteenth centuries. Before land filling occurred, the site of Fort Christian was a prominent peninsula jutting into the harbor, the logical location for defense. As originally built, the rectangular citadel enclosed the entire St. Thomas colony, including the governor's residence and the church, with projecting bastions at each corner of the fort. In 1878, when the original tower was replaced by the present Gothic-revival clocktower, the facades were also changed. Mid-eighteenth-century improvements in the range of

Fig. 266. Blackbeard's Castle, early 1680s, Charlotte Amalie, St. Thomas, U.S. Virgin Islands

Fig. 267. Bluebeard's Castle, 1689, Charlotte
Amalie, St. Thomas, U.S.V.I.

weapons, however, had rendered Fort Christian obsolete. Various functions have
since been housed here, and it was the town jail until the late 1970s. The building
now houses the Virgin Island Museum, with displays of Carib and Arawak
artifacts.

In addition to protecting their vulnerable waterfront, the early Danish
colonists in St. Thomas were concerned about the possibility of an invading force
capturing the hills above the town, from which cannon and musket fire could be
directed at the fort. To prevent this, they built small fortified watchtowers on two
of the most prominent hills above Charlotte Amalie. Trygborg, the present
Blackbeard's Castle, was constructed in the early 1680s with crude but sturdy
stonework. Frederik's Fort, now Bluebeard's Castle, was finished in 1689 and has
been incorporated into the facilities of a resort hotel.

The island of St. Croix is also the site of significant Danish forts. Fort Christiansvaern, the best preserved, was built in 1749 to protect Christiansted's harbor,
and its appearance today is relatively unchanged. The stuccoed walls are built
mainly of hard yellow ballast brick and are of relatively simple design, with horizontal emphasis obtained by the use of parapet walls and stringcourse. Crenellations in the parapet occur sparingly. The Danish army was garrisoned here until
1878, when the building became a police station and courthouse.

Fort Frederik, also on St. Croix, was erected to guard the Frederiksted harbor
from pirates and smugglers (see plate 29). Built in 1760, it has been restored to
the way it looked in 1820. Construction is stucco on stone, and its composition
is also horizontal, emphasized with stringcourses. Curved and triangular pedi-

Fig. 268. Fort Christiansvaern, 1749, Christiansted, St. Croix, U.S.V.I.

ments "float" above the windows on the north facade facing the courtyard. The arcade below has emphasized imposts and keystones. Fort Frederik claims the distinction (vied for by the fort on the island of Statia) of being the first to fire a foreign gun salute, in 1776, to the new flag of the United States of America. In 1848, the proclamation abolishing slavery in the Danish West Indies was read here by Governor General Peter Von Scholten. The fort now serves as a historical site and museum.

CHAPTER 8

PUBLIC AND INSTITUTIONAL BUILDINGS

JAMAICA

The importance of the overall composition of the Spanish Town Square has already been discussed. Although no Spanish structures survive here, the Georgian buildings with which the British replaced them are harmonious and appropriate to the setting.

The focal point of the square, in the center of the north side, is the Rodney Memorial, raised in 1790 to commemorate the victory of Admiral George Rodney in the 1782 Battle of the Saints (see plate 30). Cognizant of the French plan to invade Jamaica from Martinique, Rodney intercepted them, scoring a decisive victory. The statue, by the English sculptor John Bacon, shows Rodney in Roman tunic, the custom in statuary at that time. Flanked by two cannons from the defeated French flagship, it stands in an octagonal arcaded temple with

Fig. 269. Aerial view of Spanish Town Square, St. Catherine Parish, Jamaica

156

Rodney's coat of arms in the center arch. The other buildings on the north side of the square house the Island Record Offices.

On the west side of the square the official residence of the colonial governor, King's House, was erected in 1762. Built around two courtyards, it covered an entire city block. A large portion of King's House was badly damaged by the 1907 earthquake, and a 1925 fire consumed all but the main eastern facade and the stables. The building had been built of brick in Flemish bond, with glazed headers. The principal rooms were placed at ground level. Six Ionic columns support a classical front portico, the pediment of which displays the British coat of arms.

In 1818, the Courthouse was erected on the south side of the square, built on the site of the Spanish Church of the White Cross. Destroyed by fire in 1986, only the shell of the Courthouse remains.

At approximately the same time that King's House was built, the House of Assembly was constructed on the east side of the square in a completely different architectural style. The two buildings nevertheless complement each other across the square, with corresponding placement of central porticoes and end pavilions. The House of Assembly has an impressive brick arcade on the ground level with a deep veranda above.

A fine example of "Jamaica Georgian" is found in the Old Courthouse at Halfway Tree in St. Andrew Parish. Records indicate that, as originally built in 1807, the courthouse had ten-foot-wide timber-supported verandas on all four sides at both levels. When more interior space was needed, most of these verandas were enclosed. The exterior appearance was further altered by the

Fig. 270. King's House, 1762, Spanish Town, Jamaica, Georgian residence of the colonial governor

Fig. 271. House of Assembly, ca. 1818, Spanish Town, Jamaica

Fig. 272. Arcade, House of Assembly

Fig. 273. Old Courthouse, 1807, Halfway Tree, St. Andrew Parish, Jamaica, an example of "Jamaica Georgian"

addition of "coolers" at the windows. The building survived both the 1907 earthquake and Hurricane Gilbert in 1988.

Among a number of other handsome courthouses in Jamaica is the Manchester Courthouse in Mandeville, built about 1820. The main level is elevated, accessed by a double stairway. A modest entrance portico is supported by Tuscan columns. The building is said to have been modeled on the courthouse at Poole, Dorset, England.

St. Thomas Courthouse, in Morant Bay, has been described as a "creolized"

Fig. 274. Manchester Courthouse, ca. 1820, Mandeville, Jamaica

Fig. 275. St. Thomas Courthouse, Morant Bay, Jamaica, rebuilt after the 1865 uprising

version of the Mandeville building. The current structure is an 1867 reconstruction of the original, destroyed in an 1865 uprising. This is a significant building in Jamaican history, because the leaders of the uprising were hanged from the center arch of the gutted courthouse. Dual stairways ascend to the entrance portico, which is supported by brick arches. The building is built of stone with brick quoins. There is a small lantern on the roof.

The Portland Courthouse, 1895, dominates the square in Port Antonio. Built of brick with stone quoins, its appearance is dominated by cast-iron, two-story verandas, front and back.

Trelawny Courthouse was built in Falmouth in 1815 where a fort once stood.

Restoration after a 1926 fire considerably altered the roof design but retained the classical entrance portico, supported by four Tuscan columns. The courtroom level is elevated, reached by a double staircase.

The Trelawny Post Office is another significant nineteenth-century Falmouth building. It has an arcaded piazza over the sidewalk with emphatic quoins and stringcourse. The ridge of the shingle roof sports a typical Jamaican detail, the cap and comb.

Fig. 276. Portland Courthouse with cast-iron verandas, Port Antonio, Jamaica

Fig. 277. Trelawny Courthouse, Falmouth, Jamaica, with a classical portico

ST. KITTS

The Treasury Building in Basseterre, constructed in 1894, housed the entire administration of the island until the end of World War II. A vaulted passage that runs through the building, leading to the dock, was important as the official entry onto the island before the airport was built, when everyone arrived in St. Kitts by boat. It continues to be an active spot when the ferry arrives from the

Fig. 278. Trelawny Post Office, Falmouth, Jamaica

Fig. 279. Treasury Building, 1894, Basseterre, St. Kitts, an imposing classical presence on the waterfront

sister island of Nevis. The Treasury Building, with its formal organization and central dome, is an imposing presence on the Basseterre waterfront.

ANTIGUA

The design of the Courthouse, built in 1747, is attributed to architect Peter Harrison (see plate 31). The oldest building still in use in St. John's, it was damaged in the 1843 earthquake but restored. It is built of stone, and the arched openings on the lower floor are emphasized with quoins. Below a double stringcourse are rusticated corner pilasters. Very plain detailing occurs on the upper level. A classical pediment emphasizes the rear entrance. The building now serves as the Antigua and Barbuda Archives.

ST. LUCIA

The Police Station in Castries is a curious mixture of styles, Gothic revival in its windows and steep-pitched roof with classical emphases in its quoins and stringcourses.

The Castries Library is a carefree Victorian combination of many different architectural elements and bright colors, a delightful accent on Columbus Square (see plate 32). The front facade has a balustrade, central pediment, and flatheaded windows; the windows on the side elevation have arched heads.

Fig. 280. Police Station, Castries, St. Lucia, a curious mixture of styles

BARBADOS

Across the Inner Basin in Bridgetown lie the Public Buildings in the background of Trafalgar Square, along with the fountain and the bronze statue of Horatio Nelson. The west wing of the House of Assembly building was completed in 1872 and the east wing in 1874. A photo taken about 1882 shows a large clock tower in the east wing. This tower had to be demolished in 1884, when its foundations started to sink. In 1886, the two towers of the west wing were remodeled and the clock installed in one of these. Material for the buildings is coral

Fig. 281. Photo of Public Buildings, ca. 1882, Bridgetown, Barbados, showing clock tower in the east wing of the House of Assembly

Fig. 282. Remodeled Public Buildings, west wing, Bridgetown, Barbados

limestone, easily obtainable from Barbados quarries and used extensively in Bridgetown buildings. In the Public Buildings, Gothic-revival style is apparent in the pointed arches, the octagonal tower, and the machicolations on the parapets of both wings (see plate 33). The Gothic windows in the chamber of the Parliament building are paned with stained-glass portraits of the kings and queens of England. "Coolers" added to the exterior fit uncomfortably on the pointed-arch windows.

The Police Station in Bridgetown has some awkward detailing, particularly in the interruption of the quoins of the arch by the stringcourse. In addition, the facade is very busy, as almost every detail is emphasized.

GRENADA

When York House in St. George's was built, or what was to have been its purpose, remain unanswered questions. For many years, however, it has housed the Supreme Court on the lower floor and the Houses of Parliament above. Unusual pointed arches are combined with brick quoins and stringcourses.

TRINIDAD

In the late eighteenth century, the Spaniards and the French immigrants began quarrying stone in Port of Spain, and its use was given impetus by the arrival of the English. Unfortunately, the few examples of Georgian architecture in public buildings erected by the English are gone.

Daniel Meinerts Hahn, from Germany, was the architect of Red House in

Fig. 283. York House, St. George's, Grenada, home of Supreme Court and Houses of Parliament

Port of Spain, the second government building to bear this name. The first Red House, painted red for Queen Victoria's 1897 Diamond Jubilee, was gutted in the 1903 Water Riots and rebuilt and again painted red in 1907 (see plate 34). The design is somewhat French Renaissance in character, showing a loose kinship to Pavillon Richelieu at the Louvre, with Corinthian/composite columns and pilasters, round-head and segmental arches, and fluted jambs. Red House has pavilions at the ends and at the center; the central pavilion is taller and open vertically from floor to dome. It has a groined dome roof, balustrade, cupola, and French Renaissance dormers. There was some damage to the building in the July 1990 coup attempt.

The Port of Spain Police Headquarters, commissioned in 1876, was gutted by fire in 1882 and restored two years later (see plate 35). It is polychrome Italian Gothic revival, with machicolations in the parapet of its square tower. The major Gothic arch has interesting subdivisions, with a wheel window located above. In the attempted 1990 coup, the building was again gutted by fire.

The Royal Victoria Institute (now the National Museum), Port of Spain, was also designed by Hahn. It opened in 1892, was destroyed by fire in 1920, and rebuilt in 1923. It has a restrained lower facade with ornate curvilinear gables and roof dormers with decorative bargeboards (see plate 36). The anchor in front of the building is claimed to be the one lost by Columbus on his first voyage to Trinidad.

The Old Fire Brigade Station, in Port of Spain, displays a variety of styles. Although it has quoins and other classical details, its steep roof and scrolled fascia have Victorian overtones. There is strong horizontal emphasis, with connecting hoods over the windows and a heavy molding at the stringcourse. The dominant

Fig. 284. Old Fire Brigade Station, Port of Spain, Trinidad, a variety of styles

Fig. 285. Public Library, 1901, Port of Spain, Trinidad

tower has round-headed windows and is placed diagonally to acknowledge its position on a corner property.

The Port of Spain Public Library was constructed of brick and stone in 1901. A two-story arcade provides shaded passageways for both levels, and a pedimented projection emphasizes the center bay.

BAHAMAS

The Nassau Public Library, an octagonal building on Shirley Street, was constructed in 1799 by Joseph Eve (see plate 37). Its original use as a jail accounts for its heavy masonry construction and the stone-concrete vaulting over the first- and second-story rooms, which served as cells. The central enclosed space on the third floor was surrounded by a gallery, roofed over at a later date. The delight of the building derives primarily from its octagonal shape and from the third-floor addition with its groined dome. In form the building is reminiscent of the Magazine in colonial Williamsburg, a resemblance that may be attributable to Lord Dunmore, who was governor of Virginia before coming to Nassau. Since 1879, this unique building has served as Nassau's public library.

The three Public Buildings in Nassau are Georgian in site placement and in building design, probably influenced by the Loyalists who fled to the city in 1783 after the American War of Independence. They are symmetrically composed, the central building fronted by an axial-pedimented portico supported by four columns. The buildings resemble Governor Tryon's Palace in New Bern, North Carolina, the old capital of the Carolina colony. (As mentioned previously, when the Public Buildings were constructed in 1812 they directly overlooked the harbor, an amenity that disappeared when landfill pushed the shore line one block north.) Originally, the east (left) building housed the colonial secretary's office, treasury, and customs. The center building housed the post office, Legislative Council, courtroom, and chief justice's chambers. The House of Assembly and the offices of the attorney and surveyor general and the provost marshal were located in the west (right) building. The classical facades employ stringcourses, quoins, and shuttered windows.

Government House, on Mount Fitzwilliam in Nassau, was completed in

Fig. 286. Public Buildings, 1812, Nassau, Bahamas, Georgian in design and placement

Fig. 287. Old picture postcard of Government House, 1806, Nassau, Bahamas

1806. Also Georgian in design, the central building has a prominent center-pedimented portico to shelter arriving vehicles, supported by four Ionic columns. A cupola is prominent on the roof and, as in the Public Buildings, there are string-courses, quoins, and shuttered windows. A number of additions have been made to the original building. The east wing, including the ballroom, was built 1907–10 but was badly damaged in the 1929 hurricane. Extensive interior renovation occurred under the Duke and Duchess of Windsor in 1940.

PUERTO RICO

Alcaldía, the city hall in San Juan, was built to resemble its counterpart in Madrid. Begun in 1604, a lack of funds prolonged construction until 1789. The facade is composed of a double arcade flanked by two towers, one of which was not built until 1889. The long formal room occupying most of the second floor was for many years the center of San Juan's social life.

About the middle of the nineteenth century, the Spanish Renaissance style became popular in Puerto Rico for public buildings. A good example of this trend is the Intendency Building, built on three floors around a large interior patio. It has housed the Spanish Treasury and, in this century, the Puerto Rico Departments of the Interior, Education, Treasury, and Justice. It is now headquarters for the State Department.

Fig. 288. Alcaldía, begun 1604, completed 1789, San Juan, Puerto Rico; inspired by the city hall in Madrid

Fig. 289. Alcaldía patio

The Capitol, 1925–29, is the seat of the bicameral legislature of Puerto Rico. Although the building's form is North American, the designer was Rafael Carmoega, a pioneer among Puerto Rican–born professional architects. The Capitol seems to have been modeled after the Columbia University Library, New York City, designed by McKim, Mead, and White, and constructed in 1893. The impressive rotunda has an eighty-foot-high dome supported on pendentives. The interior mosaics and friezes, depicting important events in Puerto Rican history, were made in Italy. A back-lit stained-glass coat of arms at the top of the dome throws light upon a copy of Puerto Rico's constitution, contained in an urn in the rotunda.

El Manicomio, the old insane asylum in San Juan, has a domed central pavilion with pedimented Ionic portico. Wings on either side are fronted by arcaded passages on two levels. The building is now the School of Plastic Arts.

Casa Alcaldía, the city hall in Ponce, was the first government building in that town. When it was constructed in 1843 by the Military Corps of Engineers, it

Fig. 290. Intendency Building, San Juan, Puerto Rico, Spanish Renaissance style

Fig. 291. Intendency Building patio

Fig. 292. Capitol, 1929, San Juan, Puerto Rico, showing North American influence

Fig. 293. Capitol rotunda

Fig. 294. El Manicomio, San Juan, Puerto Rico, the old insane asylum

Fig. 295. Casa Alcaldía, 1843, city hall of Ponce, Puerto Rico

Fig. 296. Casa Alcaldía patio

held the military headquarters and a jail. The two-story building, enclosing a typical interior arcaded courtyard, continues to serve city functions, housing the offices of the mayor and of the municipal assembly.

CUBA

The distinctive eighteenth-century architecture of Cuba was based primarily on the architecture of southern Spain and was influenced by Italian neoclassicism. In the nineteenth century, more florid detail was added. After independence, Cuba experienced numerous foreign influences, including many from the United States. With the establishment of the Architecture School at the University of Havana about 1900, however, commissions were increasingly handled by local architects.

Fig. 297. Patio, Palace of the Captains General, 1792, Havana, Cuba

Fig. 298. El Templete, 1827, a classical temple, Havana, Cuba

One of the earliest Havana buildings, located on Arms Square, is the Palace of the Captains General. Completed in 1792, it was the seat of the colonial government until 1898, when Spain withdrew from the island (see plate 38). Beginning in 1902, it housed the offices of the first three presidents of the Republic. It is now the Museum of the City of Havana and the city historian's office. The facade facing Arms Square has, at street level, a nine-bay arcade with engaged Tuscan columns. The regularly spaced windows on the upper level have ornate head designs. A pediment at the parapet defines the access point into the arcaded interior patio, in the center of which is a marble statue of Christopher Columbus.

At the northeast corner of Arms Square is the neoclassic El Templete, erected in 1827 with a pedimented portico supported by Tuscan columns and Doric entablature. A symbolic ceiba tree located here marks the city's founding. Inside El Templete are three murals painted by French artist Jean Baptiste Vermay, who is buried below his work.

The Old Capitol is one of the most prominent buildings on the Prado, in Havana (see plate 39). It was originally intended to be the presidential palace, but when Mario Menocal came to power in 1913, he directed the palace to be constructed on another site and transformed the half-finished structure into the capitol. Much of the original was demolished, and the rotunda, high dome, and entrance portico were added in mimicry of the Washington, D.C., capitol. A number of architects were involved before it was finally finished in 1929, under the presidency of Gerardo Machado. After the 1959 revolution, the building ceased to serve as the capitol and became the Academy of the Sciences.

The Spanish Consulate, in Havana, is one of the most interesting consulates

Fig. 299. Spanish Consulate, Havana, Cuba, an example of monumental baroque

in the city. Its three major floors are topped by a balustrade, with two additional partial floors. The building is monumental, with the usual pedestrian arcade at street level. Windows on the upper floors have exuberant baroque head details and balustraded balconies.

DOMINICAN REPUBLIC

St. Nicholás de Bari Hospital, in Santo Domingo, was modeled after early hospitals in Spain: four building wings in a cruciform plan, converging on a rib-vaulted chapel. The hospital was founded by order of Governor Nicholás de Ovando and built 1503–8, the first stone hospital/church in the Americas. Even in ruins, it is still impressive.

The Columbus Lighthouse, 1991, is outside the time frame of this study but is included because it was conceived long ago. An international competition for its design was held in 1929, attracting 455 entries from forty-eight countries. The winning design was a recumbent cross, one-half mile long, a reminder of the wooden cross set up by Columbus when he first landed on Hispaniola. Work on the lighthouse design began in the 1930s, but Trujillo abandoned it as too extravagant. The advent of the 1992 quincentennial celebration revived interest in the project, which was built at a cost of approximately $40 million. It houses five international museums, a library, and the mausoleum of Christopher Columbus, moved here from the Santo Domingo Cathedral. The main feature of the building is a 350,000-watt lighting system, which beams a gigantic cross several miles into the night sky.

Fig. 300. Ruins of St. Nicholás de Bari Hospital, 1508, Santo Domingo, Dominican Republic, the first stone hospital/church in the Americas

Fig. 301. Columbus Lighthouse, 1991, Santo Domingo, Dominican Republic, a project revived for the 1992 quincentennial

HAITI

The Public Buildings of Haiti depend heavily on the formula of French Renaissance architecture: a long classical facade with end pavilions and a taller central entrance pavilion.

Two predecessors of the National Palace, in Port-au-Prince, were destroyed by revolutions in 1869 and in 1912. The present edifice, constructed in 1918, was designed by Georges Baussan (see plate 40). It is two floors, elevated above a basement, with monumental steps at the central pavilion. The three pavilions have groined dome roofs with a continuous balustrade along the roof line. Small dormers punctuate the roof. The entrance pavilion has a classical pedimented portico supported by four Ionic columns two stories high. Fenestration is simple and regular, and the entire building is painted white.

The Palace of Justice resembles the National Palace in its color and in its three-pavilion composition with groined dome roofs. The portico of the central pavilion is quite different, however, for it is arcaded on the lower level with columns above and a roof without the classical pediment.

The three pavilions of the Palace of the Ministries have green mansard roofs that contrast with the white building. Open two-story arcaded passageways front the two connecting segments, and the pavilions have pediments and corner pilasters. The higher entrance pavilion has a pedimented portico with supporting columns at two levels.

MARTINIQUE

The Fort-de-France city hall, Hotel de Ville, is a simple two-story rectangle with a hip roof. The facade is embellished above the stringcourse with stylized Ionic pilasters between the windows. The central pedimented pavilion projects slightly with an arcade below and corresponding arch-headed windows above. A cupola and metal cresting embellish the roof.

The Palace of Justice, in Fort-de-France, is a two-story, three-bay neoclassical building. The lower level is arcaded stone with engaged composite columns and rusticated corner pilasters. The upper level has plain wall surfaces and simple

Fig. 302. Palace of Justice, Port-au-Prince, Haiti, showing French influence

Fig. 303. Palace of the Ministries, Port-au-Prince, Haiti

pilasters. Pairs of arch-headed windows with balustrades relate to the lower arcade. Antefixae occur along the roof edge.

The Schoelcher Library, Fort-de-France, was named after Victor Schoelcher, a French statesman who was largely responsible for the emancipation of slaves in the French West Indies (see plate 41). He donated thousands of books to the library to help the ex-slave population learn to read and write. This fascinating cast-iron structure, originally an exhibit building at the 1899 World Exposition in Paris, was dismantled and shipped to Martinique for use as a library. The facade is decorated with blue, pink, green, and gold mosaics and with intricate metalwork.

Fig. 304. Hotel de Ville, Fort-de-France, Martinique, city hall

Fig. 305. Palace of Justice, Fort-de-France, Martinique, neoclassical

Fig. 306. Schoelcher Library skylight, Fort-de-France, Martinique

SINT MAARTEN

The Courthouse, in Philipsburg, was built in 1793, destroyed by a hurricane, and rebuilt in 1825 by slaves (see plate 42). It is a straightforward, robust building with a masonry lower level and frame upper portion. It is difficult to assign an architectural style to this naively delightful building, which makes only a feeble attempt at historicism with its quoins and flat arch. It serves as post office and town hall for Philipsburg.

CURAÇAO

Although Willemstad is the capital of the Netherlands Antilles, the town has always viewed itself as more mercantile than administrative, an attitude reflected in its buildings.

The Stadhuis (Town Hall), on Wilhelmina Plaza, was built in 1858 to house the Colonial Council and the Court of Justice on the upper floor, a prison on the lower level. The occupancies have since changed, although the Court of Justice still functions in this building and the Parliament of the Netherlands Antilles assembles here. The Town Hall is symmetrical about a central pedimented portico supported by four Tuscan columns. The pediment, with a roof slope much steeper than "correct" classical, displays the Dutch coat of arms.

The Government Palace is located within the quadrangle that was part of Fort Amsterdam and houses the offices of the central government of the Netherlands Antilles. Access to the governor's residence is via impressive twin staircases within the fort. Three arched openings define the entry at the upper level, and white pilasters flanking the windows add interest to the walls on either side. There are dormers in the hip roof.

Fig. 307. Stadhuis, 1858, Willemstad, Curaçao, a classical town hall

U.S. VIRGIN ISLANDS

Because Charlotte Amalie, St. Thomas, is the capital of the U.S. Virgin Islands, the major public buildings are now located in this town. Important and interesting buildings in St. Croix also deserve scrutiny, however, for the capital of the Danish West Indies was once on that island. In recent years in these islands, commercial activities have declined and government functions have increased, so that a number of structures erected to support commerce have been adapted to public purposes.

The most conspicuous building on Government Hill, Charlotte Amalie, is Government House, the fourth such building on this site. Completed in 1867, it was designed by Otto Marstrand, a St. Thomas merchant, as a meeting place for

Fig. 308. Government Palace, Willemstad, Curaçao, houses the central government of the Netherlands Antilles

Fig. 309. Government Palace, access stairs to the governor's residence

Fig. 310. Government Hill, Charlotte Amalie, St. Thomas, U.S. Virgin Islands

Fig. 311. Government House, 1867, Charlotte Amalie, St. Thomas, U.S.V.I.

Fig. 312. Lieutenant Governor's Building, Charlotte Amalie, St. Thomas, U.S.V.I.

Fig. 313. Legislative Building, 1874, Charlotte Amalie, St. Thomas, U.S.V.I., built as barracks for the Danish military

the Danish Colonial Council. The building is a simple hip-roofed rectangle of buff brick painted white. The front facade is a symmetrical three stories in seven bays. A slight parapet rises in a pedimented "gesture" over the central three bays. There is a strong dentiled stringcourse at the roof line and uniform brick rusticated pilasters at the corners. Slender cast-iron Corinthian columns support porches for the full width of the first and second levels. Intricately designed cast-iron railings grace these porches, and solid shutters flank the windows. The various floor levels are indicated on the building facades by brick stringcourses.

The ground floor contains the executive offices; the second floor, which

Fig. 314. Continental Building, 1837, Charlotte Amalie, St. Thomas, U.S.V.I., built as the Customs Offices

opens to a rear garden, contains reception areas; the third floor houses the private quarters of the governor.

The Lieutenant Governor's Building, two doors east of Government House, is a smaller three-story, seven-bay building with a strong horizontal accent. A three-bay porch with Tuscan columns emphasizes the main entrance. Another porch, like an afterthought, occurs above this on the second level.

The Legislative Building, built in 1874 on the harbor in Charlotte Amalie, has served a number of functions. Built as barracks for the Danish military, it then served this purpose for the U.S. Marines. Later, it was a public high school before becoming the seat of the Virgin Island Legislature. Its lime-green walls with white shutters reflect the Danish colors popular when the building was constructed.

The Continental Building, Charlotte Amalie, constructed in 1837, housed the main Customs Offices for St. Thomas. Its material is a striated pattern of yellow brick with a stringcourse. A rusticated arcade at street level establishes the rhythm of the windows above, which have flat-arch heads. At the roofline is another of the pediment "gestures" frequently found in Danish colonial examples. The Continental Building is now a retail space.

Government House, Christiansted, St. Croix, served at one time as the capitol of the Danish West Indies and residence of the governor general. Its impressive main staircase gave access to a spacious ballroom on the upper floor. The building was originally two separate residences, the eastern one built in 1747, and the western in 1797. The two were joined, somewhat incompatibly, in the 1830s. The U.S. District Court and the Christiansted administrator's offices are now located here.

The Danish West India and Guinea Company Warehouse, on the waterfront in Christiansted, was built in 1749. The property of the company that once both owned St. Croix and monopolized its trade, this building housed company offices, provisions, and personnel. Slaves were auctioned in the courtyard. There is simple detailing in the stuccoed masonry walls and in the hip roof. The U.S. Post Office is now located here.

Fig. 315. Government House, Christiansted, St. Croix, U.S.V.I., at one time the capitol of the Danish West Indies

Fig. 316. Danish West India and Guinea Company Warehouse, 1749, Christiansted, St. Croix, U.S.V.I., now the post office

The Old Danish Customs House, Christiansted, located near the warehouse, was completed in 1830, although a part of the first floor dates to 1751. The building is stuccoed masonry with impressive steps leading to the elevated main entrance. A sheltered arcade occurs at the ground level.

Another building important to the functioning of nineteenth-century Christiansted was the Scale House, built in 1856, where imports were inspected and weighed for tax purposes. The lower level is stuccoed masonry with emphatic quoined-arch openings. The wood-shingled wood-frame upper floor has a hip roof.

Fig. 317. Old Danish Customs House, 1830, Christiansted, St. Croix, U.S.V.I.

Fig. 318. Scale House, 1856, Christiansted, St. Croix, U.S.V.I., where imports were inspected and weighed

CHAPTER 9

RELIGIOUS BUILDINGS

During colonial times in the Caribbean, religion was primarily an activity for the European colonists, not for their slaves. Slave marriages were not permitted, and family life was discouraged because it might complicate the owners' freedom to sell their slaves.

The Anglican church, the planters' church in the English islands, largely ignored the slaves. Similarly, in the French and Spanish islands, the planters obstructed the Roman Catholic missionaries in their efforts to make converts to Christianity among the slaves, although slaves were required to be baptized. Nor, in general, were slaves allowed to practice the spiritual rituals with which they had been familiar in Africa.

When the Moravians established their first mission in the Caribbean in 1732 on the island of St. Thomas, their primary aim was to bring religion to slaves. From there, the Moravian movement spread to the other Caribbean islands.

Also resident throughout the Caribbean, as a result of the banishment edicts of Ferdinand and Isabella, were Jews who had been deported by or who had fled from Portugal and Spain. Many went to Brazil and from there to the various Caribbean islands, where they set up synagogues. Additional religions would be introduced to the area when slavery was abolished, for the institution of indentured labor brought many Asians to the Caribbean.

JAMAICA

The English practice of placing a church in each parish, the aim in the Caribbean colonies, was not usually realized. In Jamaica, five parish churches were erected, among them the Kingston Parish Church of St. Thomas, Apostle and Martyr. This church is still located where shown in the plan of Kingston drawn shortly after the earthquake of 1692, although several buildings preceded the present one, constructed in 1910. The building's significance is more historic than architectural, although it replicates the basic form of its more interesting predecessor.

Of greater architectural interest is St. James Parish Church in Montego Bay, built in 1775. Although severely damaged by the 1951 earthquake, only minor departures from the original design occurred in its restoration. Built of white limestone, the church is a Greek cross in plan with a bell tower at the west end. Except for the window subdivisions, the church is Georgian in inspiration, with classical roof slope, dentils, stringcourses, and quoins. An elaborate Palladian window occurs over the altar at the east end.

The oldest Anglican cathedral outside Great Britain is the Cathedral of the Diocese of Jamaica, in Spanish Town (see plate 43). Built in 1699 on the site of a Spanish church razed by Cromwell's soldiers, the cathedral has experienced several rebuildings and many alterations. It is a mixture of many architectural styles, combining round-headed and pointed arches, classical quoins, and medieval buttresses. The tower added in 1817 is topped with one of the few steeples to be found in the Caribbean.

Coke Methodist Church, Kingston, is named after Dr. Thomas Coke, founder of the Methodist missions in the West Indies. The building, severely damaged in the 1907 quake, was rebuilt in the neo-Gothic style of the original, although the design was changed considerably. It is red brick laid up in Flemish bond with octagonal turrets flanking the entrance and castellations on the parapet. Engaged buttresses occur between the Gothic windows with corner buttresses placed diagonally.

Unique for the Caribbean is Holy Trinity Roman Catholic Cathedral, in Kingston, in Byzantine-revival style (see plate 44). It was built in 1911 to replace another 1907 quake victim on a different site and designed by Raymond F. Almirall, a New York architect. Its main feature is an eighty-five-foot-high, copper-covered, poured-concrete dome. Round-headed windows pierce the buttressed drum that sits under the dome. On the interior, exposed pendentives support the roof structure. An attractive "modern" campanile sits remote from the church.

In 1662, the first Jews came to Jamaica from Brazil, followed by others from England, British Guiana, Surinam, Curaçao, and Germany. In 1882, the two synagogues that served the Kingston Jewish community were both destroyed by fire: the Sephardic synagogue of the Spaniards and Portuguese, and the English-German synagogue of the Ashkenazim. An attempt at amalgamation at that time

Fig. 319. St. James Parish Church, 1775, Montego Bay, Jamaica, Georgian in design

Fig. 320. Coke Methodist Church, Kingston, Jamaica, Gothic-revival style

Fig. 321. United Congregation of Israelites, Kingston, Jamaica

was unsuccessful, and both synagogues were rebuilt. When they were again destroyed in the 1907 quake, another attempt at uniting the two congregations was made, and in 1921 the United Congregation of Israelites brought together all Jamaican Jews at the synagogue at Duke and Charles Street.

The recently renovated building is constructed of reinforced concrete in a style that has been described as "approaching Spanish colonial." Although the exterior of the building is completely painted white, its form offers considerable

Fig. 322. St. Andrew's Scots Kirk, Kingston, Jamaica, an elongated octagonal plan

Fig. 323. William Knibb Baptist Church, Falmouth, Jamaica, rebuilt with public funds

detail of interest, with much surface modeling and numerous round-head arched openings and arcading. Inside, sand covers the floor, a practice also observed in Sephardic synagogues in Amsterdam, Curaçao, Panama, and the Virgin Islands, perhaps symbolizing the martyrdom of the Jews and reminding the congregation of the wandering of the Israelites through the Sinai Desert.

St. Andrew's Scots Kirk, Kingston, is an unusual elongated octagonal brick structure. Restoration after extensive 1907 quake damage replaced only three of the original four porticoes and reduced the height of the building. Two pairs of columns with terra cotta Corinthian capitals support a simple main entrance portico. Brick quoins emphasize the eight corners of the building. The impressive interior includes a gallery around three sides of the building and classical structural mahogany columns supporting the gallery and roof, the lower order being Ionic, with Corinthian above.

Two Jamaican churches are particularly related to the abolition of slavery. William Knibb, a Baptist minister, was a bold advocate of the social and economic rights of slaves and extremely unpopular with slave-owner planters. In the 1832 slave rebellion, the Falmouth Chapel where he preached was destroyed by the militia. When the replacement William Knibb Baptist Church was later demolished in the 1944 hurricane, strong community sentiment from the descendants of emancipated slaves prompted its rebuilding with public funds.

Phillippo Baptist Church, in Spanish Town, was named after James Phillippo, another minister who campaigned fearlessly for the abolition of slavery. A simple rectangle with regularly spaced windows on two levels, the building resembles a New England meetinghouse. A "gravestone" on the church grounds commemorates achievement of full emancipation in 1838, when all of the ex-slaves in the congregation gathered and buried their shackles.

The original building of the St. Elizabeth parish church at Black River, St. John the Evangelist, was built about 1700, but the date of the replacement building is uncertain. An inscription indicates that the tower foundation was laid in 1837, but it is thought that the main body was built earlier, about 1774. The church is constructed of yellow brick with limestone trim, and its configuration is reminiscent of the medieval English parish church. St. John, however, mixes Gothic and classical elements in its design. The tower has quoins and is topped with battlements and corner pinnacles. Stringcourses subdivide the tower into three equal sections, but these courses engage the Gothic windows at different

Fig. 324. Phillippo Baptist Church, Spanish Town, Jamaica, resembles New England meetinghouse

Fig. 325. St. John the Evangelist, Black River, Jamaica, reminiscent of medieval English parish church

and arbitrary positions. An apse occurs at the altar end. The pews, columns, and other interior woodwork are well crafted.

ST. KITTS

When the British took St. Kitts from the French in 1713, they changed the church the French had built in Basseterre in 1670 from Roman Catholic to Anglican. The building was badly damaged in the 1843 earthquake, and a hurricane the following year completed the demolition. A new St. George's Parish Church was erected on the same site in 1859, designed by William Slater of London (see plate 45). In 1867, it was gutted by fire but restored, and further restoration was required after minor quake damage in 1974. The building is strongly reminiscent of tenth-century Romanesque parish church architecture in England, despite its Gothic windows.

British law forbidding public worship by Roman Catholics in St. Kitts was in effect for almost 100 years, despite the continued presence of many French and some 1,500 Roman Catholic Portuguese indentured laborers. Not until four years after "free coloreds" were allowed to vote were Catholics given this privilege.

The Co-Cathedral of the Immaculate Conception in Basseterre was built in 1927 to replace an 1856 church building. Its eclectic design, by Fr. Claeys, is primarily Romanesque-revival style. The towers terminate with spires behind pediments.

Wesley Methodist Church, in Basseterre, was built in 1825. It has an extremely simple facade with handsome ashlar masonry. Its 1928 hurricane damage required extensive restoration, including a new steel roof structure.

The Moravian sect has existed in St. Kitts since 1777, when two missionaries came from Antigua. Zion Moravian Church, Basseterre, exemplifies the typical simplicity of Moravian church architecture.

Fig. 326. Co-Cathedral of the Immaculate Conception, 1927, Basseterre, St. Kitts

Fig. 327. Wesley Methodist Church, 1825, with handsome ashlar masonry, Basseterre, St. Kitts

Fig. 328. Zion Moravian Church, Basseterre, St. Kitts, typical Moravian simplicity

ANTIGUA

The twin towers of the Cathedral of St. John the Divine dominate the town of St. John's (see plate 46). This building was completed in 1848, a replica of its immediate predecessor destroyed by an earthquake in 1847. Although the building is constructed of stone, its interior is totally encased in wood, a feature credited with preventing damage during the 1974 quake. The statues of St. John the Divine and St. John the Baptist, standing on either side of the churchyard gate, are said to have been taken from a French ship bound for Dominica and brought to Antigua.

Portuguese immigrants had built a Roman Catholic church in St. John's when they arrived in the nineteenth century, and St. Joseph's, built in 1908, replaced that earlier building. The design of the newer church is primarily neo-Gothic, with pointed arches, "glued-on" machicolations, and, on the front only, engaged buttresses. Classical quoins join the buttresses at the two front corners and continue around the building at the other corners. An incompatible steeple straddles the roof at the front.

ST. LUCIA

The Roman Catholic Cathedral of the Immaculate Conception is centrally located on Columbus Square in Castries (see plates 47 and 48). It was constructed in 1895 in Italian Renaissance-revival style, with one of the largest floor areas of any church in the Caribbean. In the 1948 fire, this was the only major building in downtown Castries that escaped destruction.

Holy Trinity Anglican Church, also in Castries, was built in 1834. Constructed of brick, the church mixes medieval and classical details.

Fig. 329. St. Joseph's Roman Catholic Church, 1908, St. John's,
Antigua, a mixture of styles

Fig. 330. Holy Trinity Anglican
Church, 1834, Castries, St. Lucia,
mixes medieval and classical
details

BARBADOS

Each of the eleven parishes in Barbados, as was the original British intent, has a
church. St. Michael's Cathedral, Bridgetown, constructed in 1786, has had several predecessors. One of three Barbados churches that survived the 1831 hurricane, its design combines Romanesque, Gothic, and classical elements. The
round-headed windows have Gothic subdivisions with trefoil openings above
them. Although medieval buttresses occur along the exterior walls, classical
quoins are placed at the corners of the building. George Washington is said to
have come to worship at this site when he visited Barbados with his brother
Lawrence in 1751. The Lady Chapel behind the high altar was added in 1938.

St. Mary's Church, Bridgetown, was built in 1827 and also survived the 1831
hurricane. Its crenellated tower is somewhat reminiscent of that of St. Michael's,
but, with the exception of the tower, St. Mary's is Georgian style. Devoid of buttresses, the building has quoins at the corners and around the windows.

Following many years of anti-Catholic feeling, and even legislation against allowing the Roman Catholic church into Anglican Barbados, a priest was finally
allowed to establish a mission here. When a church built in 1848 was destroyed
by fire, arson was suspected. St. Patrick's Roman Catholic Cathedral was erected
in 1898 (see plate 49). It is essentially English Gothic-revival with pointed arches
and engaged buttresses. Quatrefoil windows occur in the clerestory, and striking
hammerbeam trusses support the high roof.

St. Matthias, in Hastings, dates from 1850 and was used as a chapel for the
nearby military garrison. The church has buttressed walls with clasping buttresses
at the corners of the building. The prominent porch on the west end acts as a
base for the squat tower, which is crenellated with corner pinnacles.

The Dutch who introduced sugar to Barbados were Jews, many of whom

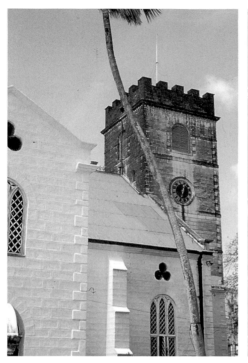 

Fig. 331. St. Michael's Cathedral, 1786, Bridgetown, Barbados, one of three Barbados churches to survive the 1831 hurricane

Fig. 332. St. Mary's Church, 1827, Bridgetown, Barbados, primarily Georgian style

Fig. 333. St. Patrick's Roman Catholic Cathedral, 1898, Bridgetown, Barbados, English Gothic-revival

Fig. 334. St. Matthias, 1850, Hastings, Barbados, built as a chapel for the nearby military garrison

Fig. 335. Barbados Synagogue, 1833, Bridgetown, design influenced by a London synagogue

decided to settle on the island. At first they were submitted to certain restrictions but in 1831 were allowed to vote and to be elected to the House of Assembly. The first Barbados synagogue, severely damaged by the 1831 hurricane, was re-built in 1833. The synagogue eventually ceased to be used and for a while was the premises of the Barbados Surf Club. Eventually it fell into severe disrepair and was dismantled. Happily, complete restoration has now occurred. The building has no true historical style but employs Gothic windows and a quasi-balustraded parapet. Its design was influenced by that of the seventeenth-century Spanish-Portuguese synagogue in the East End of London.

GRENADA

The Roman Catholic Cathedral of the Immaculate Conception in St. George's was built in 1818. It has a crenellated tower and Gothic windows.

Another crenellated tower, with corner pinnacles, gives St. Andrew's Kirk, St. George's, an English Gothic flavor.

TRINIDAD

Holy Trinity Anglican Cathedral was under construction in Woodford Square, Port of Spain, when it was discovered that it was being erected in the wrong location. Even though the walls had reached their full height, the building was demolished and a new design prepared by Philip Reinagle. The new building was completed in its new position, across the street, in 1823. Its crenellated square

Fig. 336. Roman Catholic Cathedral of the Immaculate Conception, 1818, St. George's, Grenada

Fig. 337. St. Andrew's Kirk, crenellated tower, St. George's, Grenada

Fig. 338. Holy Trinity Cathedral, 1823, Port of Spain, Trinidad, showing Gothic influence

Fig. 339. Interior, hammerbeam trusses, Holy Trinity Cathedral

tower has corner diagonal buttresses and pinnacles above. Clocks are inserted into the octagonal spire, and along the sidewalls are engaged buttresses with pinnacles. Gothic-headed windows occur between the buttresses. The handsome hammer-beam trusses on the interior were carved in England and imported to Trinidad in sections.

To serve the large Roman Catholic community in Trinidad, a result of the presence of many French and Spanish, the Gothic-revival Cathedral of the Immaculate Conception was built in 1832, also designed by Philip Reinagle (see plate 50). Construction is of blue limestone with engaged buttresses along the south and north sides. The top quarters of the twin brick octagonal towers that dominate the west front were originally stone but were replaced with wood after serious damage in an 1825 tremor.

The Abbey of Mount St. Benedict, established in 1912, is a functioning monastery in a spectacular location east of Port of Spain in the mountains of the Northern Range, overlooking the Caroni Plain. From below one sees, 800 feet up the mountainside, an informal grouping of buildings with beige walls and red tile roofs dominated by a tall campanile. The monastery began as a place of refuge for monks escaping civil unrest in Brazil, its first building a simple mud and grass ajoupa. The community is now a sizable complex, designed and constructed by Brother Gabriel Mokveld, primarily between 1938 and 1956. It includes a farm, an apiary, a school, and a rehabilitation center.

Trinidad's large Hindu and Muslim populations are the result of the 144,000 East Indian indentured laborers brought to the island between 1838 and 1918. The Jinnah Memorial Mosque, where Muslims worship in St. Joseph, is octagonal in plan (see plate 51). A high central dome is surrounded by eight

Fig. 340. Abbey of Mount St. Benedict, 1912, Trinidad, a functioning monastery

half-domes, and two minarets provide platforms from which the priest chants the call to prayer. The front arcade of the mosque employs foliated arches.

BAHAMAS

St. Matthew's Church, Nassau, constructed in 1802, is the oldest church building in the Bahamas. Located on a village green, it resembles an English country church. It was designed by Joseph Eve, a Loyalist settler, a simple rectangle with nave and side aisles separated by circular stone Ionic columns under a hip roof. Its outstanding feature is an octagonal tower and spire at the west end, added in 1816. Stained glass windows were installed between 1863 and 1876, and an enlargement in 1887 added a vestry room, organ chamber, and new chancel. Interior light is provided on the sides by large arch-headed windows provided with shutters.

Another Nassau church designed by Joseph Eve is Christ Church Cathedral, completed in 1840 and occupying the site of three early smaller churches. Its dominant square tower has corner diagonal buttresses topped by pinnacles. Inside, round stone columns support handsome timber trusses. An unusual tripartite roof defines the nave and the two side aisles. Tall Gothic windows along the sides are protected by tilting shutters. The church was enlarged in 1865 and added stained-glass windows in 1868, replaced in 1945 after being damaged.

Among the 1,500 Loyalists who fled America for the Bahamas were a considerable number of Scottish descent, whose presence led to the formation of St. Andrew's Presbyterian Church (the Kirk), begun in 1810, making it the second-

Fig. 341. St. Matthew's Church, 1802, Nassau, the oldest church building in the Bahamas

Fig. 342. Christ Church Cathedral, 1840, Nassau, Bahamas, with a dominant square tower

oldest church building on New Providence Island. It was remodeled in 1822; the belfry was erected in 1844; and enlargement occurred in 1864. The spire, added in 1847, was destroyed in the 1866 hurricane. A neo–Gothic Sunday school hall adjoins the church, which employs both pointed and round–headed arches in combination with medieval crenellations on the parapets.

St. Agnes' Parish Church, in Grant's Town, was built in 1868 with hammer-beam trusses supporting the roof over a spacious chancel. Subsequent additions included the Our Lady's Chapel in 1906 and the west porch in 1916. The design of the church is unusual Gothic revival.

A vigorous sponge industry in the Bahamas attracted a number of Greeks to the islands and led to the formation of the Greek Orthodox Church of the Annunciation, in Nassau, in 1932. The church building is small, with a simple facade and a wood-frame octagonal Byzantine tower with groined dome.

Fig. 343. Interior, Christ Church Cathedral, where round stone columns support timber trusses

Fig. 344. St. Andrew's Presbyterian Church, 1810, Nassau, Bahamas, serves many people of Scottish descent

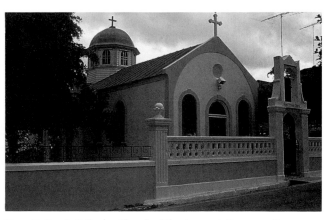

Fig. 345. St. Agnes' Parish Church, 1868, Grant's Town, Bahamas, an unusual Gothic-revival design

Fig. 346. Greek Orthodox Church of the Annunciation, 1932, Nassau, Bahamas, with Byzantine tower

Fig. 347. St. Francis Xavier Cathedral, 1887, Nassau, the first Roman Catholic church erected in the Bahamas

St. Francis Xavier Cathedral, completed in 1887, was the first Roman Catholic church erected in the Bahamas. A long, simple, neo-Gothic masonry building with buttressed walls, it has dissimilar towers centrally located along the east and west walls and a small cupola on the south end of the wood-shingle gable roof. Demarara shutters provide sun protection for the pointed-arch windows.

PUERTO RICO

The whole ecclesiastical discipline of Spain was transferred to its colonies, and the Caribbean colonies offer authentic and rare examples of medieval church architecture in the New World. One of these is San Juan Cathedral, with its display of stone vaulting (see plate 52). Built in 1540, it has suffered various disasters, including looting by the Earl of Cumberland and the loss of its roof in a hurricane. It was considerably reworked in the nineteenth century and restored in the late 1970s. The main facade of the cathedral shows Italian baroque influence, and the interior of the main dome has an interesting trompe l'oeil treatment.

Construction of San José Church, San Juan, began in 1523. Originally a Dominican chapel, it was designed by friars of that order and used Gothic stone vaults in the original section. When all monasteries were closed in Puerto Rico about 1838, this church was abandoned for a time but was later given to the Jesuit fathers, who repaired it. San José was the family church of the descendants of Ponce de León; his grave was here until 1908, when his body was moved to the cathedral. A bronze statue of Ponce de León stands in the plaza.

Fig. 348. San Juan Cathedral, 1540, San Juan, Puerto Rico, main dome interior

Fig. 349. San José Church, begun 1523, San Juan, Puerto Rico

Fig. 350. San José Church interior, ribbed dome

Santo Cristo Chapel, San Juan, is a small chapel built in Spanish Mission style with bells in a pierced gable. According to legend, at a 1753 patron saints festivity a youthful rider in a horseracing event lost his life when he failed to make the turn at the south end of Cristo Street and plunged over the precipice. A commemorative niche containing a crucifix was placed at this site, later replaced by a chapel.

Friars began construction of the Dominican Convent in 1523. The building has served many purposes during its lifetime and is now the headquarters of the Institute of Puerto Rican Culture. Arcaded galleries on its two floors enclose a large interior patio now used for various cultural activities. Works of the Dominican order are collected in the library, and the chapel houses a museum.

The three-story Convent of the Carmelite Nuns dates from 1651 and was vacated in 1903. Because of its rapid deterioration, it was threatened with demolition. In 1983, however, restoration into adaptive use as the 100-room Gran Hotel El Convento was completed. Arcaded walkways surround an interior courtyard and provide entrance into the hotel rooms. The original chapel is now a large salon with a fifty-foot domed ceiling.

The most famous landmark in San Germán is the Porta Coeli (Gate of Heaven) Church constructed in 1606 on a knoll facing a plaza, the first chapel in the Americas. In its recent restoration, original windows and niches were uncovered. The whitewashed simplicity of Porta Coeli is thought to typify the original small churches on the island. Wooden doors are set into a central large arched entrance flanked by pilasters supporting an entablature. A bell in a pierced gable crowns the symmetrical front facade. The building is now a museum of religious art.

In Ponce, the Plaza las Delicias is dominated by the Cathedral of Our Lady of Guadalupe, named for Ponce's patron saint. Built in 1670 from a design by

Fig. 351. Santo Cristo Chapel, San Juan, Puerto Rico, in Spanish Mission style

Fig. 352. Gran Hotel El Convento, San Juan, Puerto Rico, an adaptive use of an abandoned 1651 convent

Fig. 353. Gran Hotel El Convento courtyard

Fig. 354. Porta Coeli Church, 1606, San Germán, Puerto Rico, now a museum

Fig. 355. Cathedral of Our Lady of Guadalupe, 1670, Ponce, Puerto Rico, with twin west towers

Fig. 356. Cathedral of Our Lady of Guadalupe, interior vaults

Francisco Porrata Doria, it was restored in 1835 and again after the 1918 earthquake. The neoclassical west facade has twin towers. The interior is dominated by quadripartite vaults.

CUBA

Although the colonial church architecture of Cuba may not have achieved the importance of that in Mexico or Peru, it is among the most impressive church architecture in the Caribbean, combining Spanish, Mudéjar, and Creole characteristics and employing stone vaults and domes.

The Cathedral of Havana dominates the plaza on which it stands (see plate 53). Built in a number of stages, it was completed about 1777 and was then known as San Ignacio Church. It was consecrated as a cathedral in 1789. The entrance facade is heavily sculptured baroque with complicated pediments. It is symmetrical except for the towers: the considerably larger one contains the bells. In the rectangular interior, great columns separate the nave and the side aisles, each of which has four chapels. A dome dominates the interior space.

San Carlos Seminary, behind the cathedral, has been training theologians, priests, and philosophers since 1772. The baroque entrance facade is incorporated into the long elevation of the seminary, its height equal to that of the three stories of rooms on either side.

Santo Angel Custodio Church, erected 1689 on Angel Hill in Havana, was originally designed in the baroque style, although 1868 alterations changed its appearance. Exterior Gothic elements, particularly the pinnacles on the main volume and on the tower, add a vertical accent that was not an original characteristic. Interior alterations, in particular the carved mahogany altars with Gothic spires, occurred at the same time. There is clerestory lighting in the nave, with flying buttresses over the side aisles. The building was restored in 1986.

Santísima Virgen de Regla Church, across the bay from Havana in Regla, has a severely classical exterior with a single tower centrally located over the en-

Fig. 357. San Carlos Seminary, Havana, Cuba, baroque facade

Fig. 358. Santo Angel Custodio Church, 1689, Havana, Cuba, Gothic added in 1868

Fig. 359. Santo Cristo del Buen
Viaje Church, completed ca. 1760,
Havana, Cuba, with twin octag-
onal towers

trance. It is famous for its wooden image of the black Virgin of Regla holding a
white Christ child. Copied from a fifth-century African figure, it has been in the
church since 1696.

Santo Cristo del Buen Viaje Church, on Christ Square in Havana, was begun
about 1750 and completed ten years later. It has a cruciform plan and a restrained
facade. Twin octagonal towers flank a formal central arched entrance, above
which is an exterior balcony. In a recessed wall above is a rectangular window
within a blind arch, with the facade terminating in a broken pediment.

The Church and Convent of Belén, in Havana, was constructed near the end
of the seventeenth century and occupied by friars of the order of San Diego de
Alcalá until 1842, when they were evicted by officials of the Spanish government, who then moved into the convent. The church has a neoclassical front
with an unusual pierced parapet over the central curved pediment. Heavy quoins
occur on the single tower, which is set to one side. A single central entrance is
flanked by engaged columns.

Santa Clara Convent, a walled religious compound, was built between 1638
and 1643. Its nuns were aristocratic daughters who brought with them a dowry
and two slaves when they entered. The self-sufficient complex covers three
acres in the center of Havana, its two-story exterior wall severe on the street
side with few openings. Inside the enclosure, all spaces open onto generous interior galleries with open masonry arcades below and wood colonnades above.

Latin America, the building was converted, in turn, into a theater, a royal tobacco warehouse, and public offices and then left to deteriorate. In 1955, it was restored as the final resting place for the nation's heroes. The central stone dome is supported on pendentives. The enormous bronze chandelier hanging from the dome was donated to Generalissimo Rafael Trujillo by Generalissimo Francisco Franco, who also provided the iron gates, said to have belonged to a Nazi prison.

The first monastery in the New World was the Convent of San Francisco, built 1504–47. Situated on a hill overlooking Santo Domingo were the three main areas: the church, the Chapel of the Third Order (Maria de Toledo

Fig. 366. Cathedral of Santa Maria la Menor, 1541, Santo Domingo, Dominican Republic, a mixture of medieval, Renaissance, and Mudéjar styles

Fig. 367. North elevation, Cathedral of Santa Maria la Menor

Fig. 368. Pantéon Nacional, 1745, Santo Domingo, Dominican Republic, originally a church, now a mausoleum for the nation's heroes

Fig. 369. Interior, Pantéon Nacional, dome on pendentives

Chapel), and the monastic area. These buildings, now in ruins, were surrounded by ample gardens and green areas.

The Church of San Miguel, Santo Domingo, is a sixteenth-century complex where the Spanish writer Tirso de Molina (Fr. Gabriel de Téllez) wrote his *Don Juan*.

Santo Domingo's first nonsectarian school, Escuela Normal, where future teachers were trained, was founded at the end of the nineteenth century. The Chapel of the Third Dominican Order, built in the eighteenth century, became the school chapel during colonial days.

Regina Angelorum (Queen of Angels) Convent, Santo Domingo, was built in the sixteenth century and modified in the seventeenth and eighteenth centuries. It is renowned for the altarpiece above the main altar. Inside is the tomb of Padre Billini, who discovered the remains of Columbus in 1877.

The Church and Hospital of San Lázaro (St. Lazarus), Santo Domingo, was built in the sixteenth century as an asylum for those suffering from leprosy. It is claimed that a grandson of Christopher Columbus died here.

The Chapel of Our Lady of Carmen (Carmelite Church), Santo Domingo, was built in the eighteenth century. Inside is the image of the Nazarene, a Christ-like figure that holds the rank of colonel in the Dominican army.

The Chapel of San Andrés, Santo Domingo, was once part of a hospital by the same name. When that hospital was demolished and the Padre Billini Hospital was built, a portion of the original Chapel of San Andrés was retained and incorporated into the new hospital structure.

Fig. 370. Convent of San Francisco, 1504–47, Santo Domingo, Dominican Republic, now in ruins

Fig. 371. Church of San Miguel, sixteenth century, Santo Domingo, Dominican Republic

Fig. 372. Chapel of the Third Dominican Order, eighteenth century, Santo Domingo, Dominican Republic, later the school chapel for Escuela Normal

Fig. 373. Regina Angelorum Convent, sixteenth century, Santo Domingo, Dominican Republic, modified in the seventeenth and eighteenth centuries

Fig. 374. Church and Hospital of San Lázaro, sixteenth century, Santo Domingo, Dominican Republic, an asylum for those suffering from leprosy

Fig. 375. Chapel of Our Lady of Carmen, eighteenth century, Santo Domingo, Dominican Republic

Fig. 376. Chapel of San Andrés, Santo Domingo, Dominican Republic

Fig. 377. Chapel of Our Lady of Remedies, a private chapel for the Davila family, Santo Domingo, Dominican Republic

The Chapel of Our Lady of Remedies (Remedios Chapel), Santo Domingo, was a private chapel for the Davila family.

The sixteenth-century Church of Santa Barbara, located in the Santo Domingo neighborhood of seamen and stonemasons, is where Juan Pablo Duarte, one of the three founders of the Dominican Republic, was baptized. Its eclectic architecture attests to its continuous remodeling during five centuries.

HAITI

Roman Catholicism has long been the predominant religion in Haiti, a result of its settlement by Spaniards and later colonization by the French. In addition, when Christophe had himself declared King Henri I of Haiti in 1811 he established Catholicism as the state religion. Despite the current population's claim to be 80 percent Roman Catholic, voodoo derived from African rites and brought to Haiti by slaves continues to be a strong religious tradition. Haitians see no contradiction between Christianity and these voodoo practices. Creole is frequently the language of the mass, which is often accompanied by voodoo drums.

One of the most prominent buildings in Port-au-Prince is the Roman Catholic Notre Dame Cathedral, built in the early 1900s to replace the cathedral built in 1720 and since demolished (see plate 55). The present cathedral was one of the first reinforced-concrete structures in Haiti. The design of its west twin towers is reminiscent of the domes of Sacre Coeur in Paris. The interior displays quadripartite ribbed-groin vaulting.

Holy Trinity Episcopal Cathedral, Port-au-Prince, was designed by Daniel Brun and completed in 1929. Although its design is lackluster, the cathedral is famous for the frescoes on its interior walls (see plate 56). These depict biblical

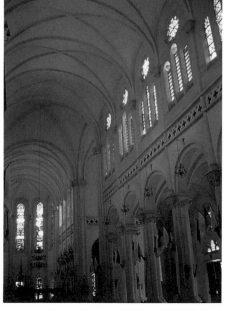

Fig. 378. East End, Notre Dame Cathedral, early 1900s, Port-au-Prince, Haiti

Fig. 379. Interior vaulting, Notre Dame Cathedral

Fig. 380. Holy Trinity Episcopal Cathedral, 1929, Port-au-Prince, Haiti

Fig. 381. Notre Dame Cathedral, 1878, Cap Haïtien, Haiti

scenes in Haitian settings and were done by more than a dozen local artists. The scenes include voodoo figures and a chicken thief being chased by a policeman. Conceived by Anglican bishop Charles Alfred Voegeli, this artwork is credited with encouraging, if not igniting, the Haitian art boom.

The original Notre Dame Cathedral in Cap Haïtien, designed by French architects in 1784, was destroyed in the 1842 quake and rebuilt in 1878 according to the design of a U.S. architect.

MARTINIQUE

One of the most unusual Caribbean churches is the Roman Catholic St. Louis Cathedral in Fort-de-France (see plate 57). Built in 1895 from a design by Gustave Eiffel, despite its Romanesque-revival style its structure is cast iron, including even the flying buttresses. The lack of clerestories between the nave and side aisles creates the effect of a "hall church" with a gallery.

Set in the forest outside Fort-de-France is Sacre Coeur de Balata, inspired by Sacre Coeur, Paris. The color is the same and the central dome has a similar shape and is also supported on an arcade, but the remainder of the design is distinctive.

GUADELOUPE

The Roman Catholic Church of St. Peter and St. Paul is the most prominent church in Pointe-au-Pitre (see plate 58). Its masonry exterior has been influenced by the Italian baroque design of Il Gesu, Rome, but the interior is nineteenth-century cast iron.

SINT MAARTEN

The Methodist Church in Philipsburg is a simple rectangular meetinghouse-type building with a wood shingle exterior. A small cupola sits on the gable roof over the entrance. Its shuttered Gothic-headed windows with complicated subdivisions offer considerable contrast to the basic building design.

Fig. 382. Interior, St. Louis Cathedral, 1895, Fort-de-France, Martinique

Fig. 383. Sacre Coeur de Balata, Martinique

Fig. 384. Methodist Church, Philipsburg, Sint Maarten, a meetinghouse type

CURAÇAO

Roman Catholic missionary work in Curaçao dates from 1526, but the earliest surviving church on the island is the Basilica of St. Anna, in the Otrobanda section of Willemstad, built in 1752. This eclectic building claims to be one of the smallest basilicas in the world. Its complicated exterior creates a fortresslike quality, derived from the crenellated square tower and the various stepped gables. A contrasting white-and-gray color scheme further complicates the exterior. Interesting cast-iron columns occur on the interior.

Although in 1763 the West India Company got permission to restore its Protestant church in Fort Amsterdam, the company instead built a completely new one, Fort Church. Its position inside the fort is reinforced by its design against siege, including a cistern and plenty of storage space for food in a vaulted cellar. The dryness of its attic allowed the sails of merchant vessels to be stored there. An exterior monumental staircase rose above the cellar, providing entry into the church. Four thick columns, freestanding on the interior, supported the roof. Brass chandeliers, a mahogany pulpit, and an awned governor's bench enhanced the otherwise stark interior. The exterior is embellished with a cannonball, embedded in the front wall by Captain William Bligh in 1804.

In 1651, the West India Company gave Joao de Illan of Amsterdam permission to take fifty Jews with him to Curaçao, and the congregation of Mikve Israel-Emanuel Synagogue was founded that year in Willemstad. This community was soon joined by Portuguese Sephardic Jews from Brazil. The present building, dating from 1733 and the oldest synagogue in continuous use in the Western hemisphere, resembles the distinctive style of synagogues in old Amsterdam (see plate 59). Curvilinear gables occur in front of a tripartite roof, from which rainwater is drained by scuppers brought through the end walls into

Fig. 385. Basilica of St. Anna, 1752, Willemstad, Curaçao, with a complicated exterior

Fig. 386. Fort Church, 1763, Willemstad, Curaçao, built to resist siege

Fig. 387. Interior, Fort Church, with four free-standing columns that support the roof

Fig. 388. Mikve Israel—Emanuel Synagogue entrance, Willemstad, Curaçao

downspouts on the faces of the building. These downspouts become strong vertical design elements on the facade, appearing almost like pilasters. Rows of small arch-headed windows with blue glass admit limited daylight to the interior. As in the Kingston, Jamaica, synagogue, sand on the floor is probably meant to remind the congregation of the wandering of the Israelites through the Sinai. The sand also has a less universal significance that relates to the time in Portugal

Fig. 389. Mikve Israel—Emanuel Synagogue
interior

Fig. 390. Temple Emanu-El, 1864, Willemstad,
Curaçao, later a theater-tavern

when the Sephardic Jews had to worship in secrecy and put down sand to muffle
the sound of their footsteps.

Another temple, Emanu-El, was built in 1864 by a group that had seceded
from the original Jewish community to become one of the first Reform congregations in the Americas. In 1964, however, a change in the ritual at Mikve
Israel-Emanuel, which combined Reconstructionist and Reform elements with
the Sephardic rite, allowed the Temple Emanu-El congregation to rejoin the
more orthodox group in their 1733 synagogue. The Temple Emanu-El building
was then sold and converted into a theater-tavern.

U.S. VIRGIN ISLANDS

In the earliest years of the Danish colonization of the West Indies, all church services were held within the still-unfinished Fort Christian on St. Thomas, where
attendance was required for all settlers regardless of faith. The Lutheran church
was the Danish state religion, and during the first decades of colonization only
Lutheran and Calvinist services were permitted.

The Church of Our Lord God of Sabaoth, in Christiansted, was St. Croix's
first Lutheran church, erected 1750–53. The building was a simple hip-roof rectangle with a molded gutter that looked like a stringcourse just below the eave-
line. By contrast with this simplicity, a tower with steeple added in the 1790s had
multiple contrasting stages topped by an octagonal cupola. No longer used as a
church, the building became a bakery, then a storehouse; it is now a museum,
the Steeple Building.

St. John's Anglican Church, in Christiansted, 1849–58, is a neo-Gothic-style stone building with a tall central tower at the entrance end. Corner buttresses topped with pinnacles occur at the corners of the building and the tower. There are crenellations on the parapets of the gable ends. Exposed wood trusses define an interesting interior volume.

Frederik Lutheran Church in Charlotte Amalie, St. Thomas, replaced two structures on this site lost to fire in 1750 and 1789. Built in 1793 in neoclassical

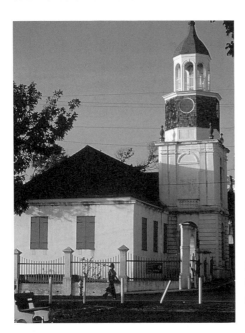

Fig. 391. Church of Our Lord God of Sabaoth, 1753, Christiansted, St. Croix, U.S. Virgin Islands, now a museum; tower and steeple added in the 1790s

Fig. 392. St. John's Anglican Church, 1849–58, Christiansted, St. Croix, U.S.V.I., neo-Gothic style

Fig. 393. Interior, St. John's Anglican Church

style, this building was also gutted by fire in 1825. When it was rebuilt in the following year, some Gothic-revival features were added. The interior has handsome antique chandeliers and eighteenth-century Danish ecclesiastical silver.

When the Danes eventually needed to attract colonists from other Caribbean islands, they developed a pragmatic tolerance of other religions. The Moravians were allowed to establish slave missions here, and a number of Moravian churches remain in the Virgin Islands. The Moravian Memorial Church on Norre Gade,

Fig. 394. Frederik Lutheran Church, 1793 and 1826, Charlotte Amalie, St. Thomas, U.S.V.I.

Fig. 395. Gothic additions, Frederik Lutheran Church

in Charlotte Amalie, was built in 1882 to commemorate the 150th anniversary of the Moravian presence in the Danish colony. A considerable departure from the usual Moravian rural simplicity, its stone finishes, pedimented door and window openings, and rusticated quoins give it an imposing urban character.

Diplomatic dealings with Catholic Puerto Rico in time led the Danes to permit a priest to come to the Danish West Indies. The Roman Catholic Cathe-

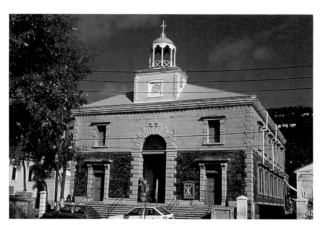

Fig. 396. Moravian Memorial Church, 1882, Charlotte Amalie, St. Thomas, U.S.V.I., built to commemorate the 150th anniversary of the Moravian presence in the Danish colony

Fig. 397. Roman Catholic Cathedral of Sts. Peter and Paul, 1848, Charlotte Amalie, St. Thomas, U.S.V.I., in mixed architectural styles

Fig. 398. St. Thomas Reformed Church, 1844, Charlotte Amalie, St. Thomas, U.S.V.I., an imitation Roman temple

Fig. 399. All Saints Anglican Cathedral, mid-nineteenth century, Charlotte Amalie, St. Thomas, U.S.V.I., Gothic revival

Fig. 400. Main entrance, All Saints Anglican Cathedral

dral of Sts. Peter and Paul, in Charlotte Amalie, was consecrated as a parish church in 1848 on the site of several earlier churches destroyed by fire and one badly damaged in the hurricane of 1837. The architectural decorations of the cathedral mix a number of styles, with Gothic-revival features dominating. What appears to be stone vaulting on the interior is actually plaster on wood lath. The columns also have wood cores. The cathedral has an impressive large white marble altar and excellent interior woodwork.

Sephardic Jews also came to the Danish West Indies and established a synagogue, replaced in 1833 by the Synagogue of Beracha Veshalon Vegmiluth Hasidim, on Crystal Gade in Charlotte Amalie. The building is a blend of Gothic revival and neoclassical, with a pointed-arch doorway as the main entrance. Except for the exterior masonry walls, it is a wood structure. Plaster coatings resembling stone disguise the structural wood columns as well as the beams between them, and as in the Catholic cathedral, the ribbed vault here is not stone but plaster on lath fastened to an elaborate roof structure.

St. Thomas (formerly Dutch) Reformed Church, Charlotte Amalie, is an imitation Roman temple constructed in 1844. Surprisingly, it is a half-timber structure using masonry infill, all covered over with stucco grooved and colored to resemble sandstone. The frontal exterior columns are timber covered with masonry.

All Saints Anglican Cathedral, Charlotte Amalie, is mid-nineteenth-century Gothic revival that has been much altered. The main entrance, now an insignificant depressed door on the east, was originally on the west elevation.

pinnacled gables and dormers, rusticated round-headed arches, quoins on corner pilasters, and a domical vault on the clock tower.

The first university in Cuba was the Royal and Papal University of San Jerónimo, founded in 1768 in Old Havana. In 1902, however, the school moved to a new section of the city and was renamed the University of Havana. A grand staircase ascends the hill to a "Roman temple" entry to the campus. The classical pediment and entablature of this building are supported by four Ionic columns *in antis.* The founding of the School of Architecture about 1900 was an important milestone in the development of a Cuban architectural expression.

THEATERS AND PLACES OF ENTERTAINMENT

Two previous theaters have occupied the site of the Ward Theatre at North Parade in Kingston, Jamaica. The Kingston Theatre, constructed in 1774, was replaced by the Theatre Royal in 1838, but it was destroyed in the 1907 quake. Colonel Charles Ward, then custos (political head of the parish) of Kingston, presented the Ward Theatre to the city in 1912.

The current building is the centerpiece of North Parade, with a large arched opening centered in its symmetrical facade. Pilasters define two bays on either side of this entrance. The building pediment is highly ornamented with oval windows, swags, and blind balustrades. Blue and white paint further accentuates the decorative elements.

The Fox Delicias Theater, in Ponce, Puerto Rico, was designed in art deco style in 1931 by Francisco Porrata Doria. It has been restored and successfully adapted for use as a shopping mall and café theater.

Fig. 405. Ward Theatre, 1912, Kingston, Jamaica, the centerpiece of the north Parade area

El Casino, San Juan, Puerto Rico, built in 1917, was the center of high-society cultural and social life on the island. Its French baroque exterior with copper cupola demonstrated an opulence appropriate to its function. A large white ballroom was the major interior space. In 1930, the Institute of Puerto Rican Culture moved its offices here; it is now a reception center for the Puerto Rican State Department, having been restored in 1984.

The most spectacular building on the Prado, Havana, Cuba, is García Lorca, the Great Theater of Havana (see plate 61). Completed in 1837, it is still a glittering setting for performances by ballet, opera, and light opera companies. This baroque-revival building has a continuous pedestrian arcade at street level. Above this rises a building that is embellished with round corner towers, statuary, balustraded balconies, and stained glass. The facade terminates at the roofline in parapets and pediments that defy further elaboration. A double staircase in the lobby provides a grand entrance into the theater.

Another interesting Cuban theater, located on La Vigía Square in Matanzas, the Sauto Theater was built in 1863 at the height of Matanzas's cultural effervescence and hosted such luminaries as actress Sarah Bernhardt and dancer Anna Pavlova. From the exterior, the theater appears to be a two-story building. A projecting pedimented element provides, at street level, an arcaded entry. The horseshoe-shaped interior has three balconies with cast-iron columns and railings. A 1969 restoration retained the original seats and fixtures, which had come from the United States.

No longer functioning as a theater, Cinelandia, in Willemstad, Curaçao, is a reminder of the days when even Curaçao built a few monuments to art deco.

Fig. 406. Fox Delicias Theater, 1931, Ponce, Puerto Rico, in restored art deco

Fig. 407. Lobby, Garcia Lorca, 1837, Havana, Cuba, a glittering setting for performances

Fig. 408. Sauto Theater, 1863, Matanzas, Cuba, host of nineteenth-century stage luminaries

Fig. 409. Horseshoe-shaped interior, Sauto Theater

TOURISM, HOTELS, AND APARTMENTS

In 1889, the idea of an 1891 Jamaica International Exhibition was proposed, and the Jamaica Hotels Law was passed in 1890 in anticipation of the expected rush of visitors. Under this law, the government offered a guarantee of the principle, with interest at 3 percent, to companies that would construct and operate hotels to the satisfaction of a government surveyor. A number of builders took advantage of the terms offered by the government, but the earthquake of 1907 took its toll of the hotels they built in the Kingston area. Only the luxurious 1890 Constant Spring Hotel exists from this era, and it now functions as a school. The exposition was held on what is now the Wolmer School grounds, Kingston. The

Fig. 410. Old photo, Jamaica International Exhibition of 1891, Kingston, in eclectic Moorish style

Fig. 411. Old picture postcard, Royal Victoria Hotel, 1861, Nassau, Bahamas, a profitable place during the U.S. Civil War

1891 temporary exposition building was eclectic Moorish style, complete with minarets.

The 200-room Marine Hotel, Hastings, Barbados, was built in 1887 by George Whitfield. Architecturally famous for its ornate cast-iron balustrades, spacious verandas, and huge ballroom, since 1972 it has been used as offices by the Barbados government.

The Bahamian prosperity that accompanied the U.S. Civil War led planners to expand their original design for the Royal Victoria Hotel, Nassau, completed in 1861. Built by the Bahamas government, the four-story building was set in luxurious tropical gardens. During the Civil War it was patronized primarily by

Fig. 412. Royal Victoria ruins,
after 1990 fire

blockade runners and by officers of the Confederate Army and was extremely profitable. In 1898, H. M. Flagler purchased it from the government, completely renovated and enlarged it, and added wide verandas and more elaborate landscaping of the spacious gardens. After a gradual demise, it closed in 1971, and in 1990 it burned, leaving only segments of the masonry walls.

The first Hotel Colonial, in Nassau, owned by H. M. Flagler, was completed in 1901 and destroyed by fire in 1922. On its site the Bahamas government built the New Colonial Hotel the following year, which was sold to Sir Harry Oakes and renamed the British Colonial Hotel. It occupies the site of Fort Nassau, the city's earliest fort. The waterfront building elevation is axial/symmetrical Spanish colonial baroque, similar in style to contemporary South Florida buildings.

Hotel Melía, in the center of historic Ponce, Puerto Rico, was built in 1908 and is the oldest hotel in Puerto Rico. Its two-story facade is restrained classical-revival style. Regularly spaced openings are separated by shallow pilasters, which are interrupted by a heavy cornice and terminate at a balustraded parapet.

The six-story Miami Apartment building in the Condado section of San Juan, Puerto Rico, was constructed in 1936 from the design of architect Pedro Méndez, who had been educated in the United States. It employs the design characteristics of art deco, with pastel colors and small geometric designs. Strong curves are used in the corner balconies and in the glass-block panels that continue the full height of the building.

The Hotel Normandie, another art deco structure in San Juan, was designed by Raul Richard and built in the early 1940s. It is triangular in plan with a semicircular "apse" facing the street. Heavy horizontal projections emphasize the floor lines.

Ponce was the site of Puerto Rico's Exposition-Fair, which attracted visitors from all over the island. Its main building, constructed in 1883, was to become

Fig. 413. British Colonial Hotel, 1923, Nassau, Bahamas, occupies the site of Fort Nassau

Fig. 414. Miami Apartments, 1936, San Juan,
Puerto Rico, in pastel art deco

Fig. 415. Hotel Normandie, early 1940s, San Juan,
Puerto Rico, deco with triangular plan

the home of Ponce's Fireman's Corps (see plate 62). Named Parque de Bombas, this garish red-and-black structure is Ponce's most famous landmark and in 1990 became a museum of memorabilia of the history of the city and its volunteer fire brigade.

In Cuba, a former hotel now provides the shell for the Havana Sports Hall. It is interesting from the standpoint of adaptive use, as it has retained only the street facades of the original building, the interior of which had collapsed. An enormous roof structure for the new facility rises above the original three-story walls, and trussed connections anchor the old facades to the new structure.

The Inglaterra Hotel is the oldest hotel in current use in Havana, dating from the 1880s. Pedestrian traffic along Prado is accommodated under the colonnade that fronts the hotel at street level, and three floors of hotel rooms occur above this. The street elevation is ornate, with baroque pediments above the French

Fig. 416. Interior, Parque de Bombas, Ponce, Puerto Rico

Fig. 417. Havana Sports Hall, Cuba; its shell once enclosed a hotel

doors, which open from the hotel rooms onto cast-iron balconies. The facade is accented by pilasters and crowned by swag ornaments and a balustrade. The interior public spaces are elegantly restored, showing high decorative ceilings, iron grillwork, stained glass, and Moorish details.

San Miguel, a small Cuban town, is known primarily because it was at one time the fashionable place to go to "take the waters." Legend has it that a slave named Miguel was cured of a fatal illness by bathing in the spring waters in this

Fig. 418. Inglaterra Hotel, 1880s, oldest hotel in Havana, Cuba, in current use

Fig. 419. Interior, Inglaterra Hotel

location that would later bear his name. In 1926, the San Miguel Baños Hotel was constructed on the grounds of the springs (see plate 63). The symmetrically formal building has a monumental central exterior stairway that leads to an open balustraded terrace. From this, three arched openings lead into a spacious ballroom. Domed towers accent the four corners of the building. The springhouses are romantic enclosures in a variety of exotic styles.

The Office of Tourism in Pointe-au-Pitre, Guadeloupe, is a handsome 1927 two-story building. Colonnaded walkways with balustrades occur outside both levels on the two street sides of the building. The enclosure proper is composed entirely of arch-headed double doors along these two sides.

Fig. 420. One of the spring-houses at San Miguel Baños Hotel, San Miguel, Cuba

Fig. 421. Office of Tourism, 1927, Pointe-au-Pitre, Guadeloupe

Fig. 422. Grand Hotel, 1843, Charlotte Amalie, St. Thomas, U.S. Virgin Islands, now houses shops, offices, and a restaurant

Grand Hotel, in Charlotte Amalie, St. Thomas, U.S. Virgin Islands, was built in 1843. Originally a three-story building, its top floor was destroyed by a hurricane and fire. In 1975, it ceased to be a hotel and has since experienced adaptive uses, with shops on the ground floor and offices in the former guest rooms. These upper-story rooms open either onto an exterior cast-iron balcony or an arcaded open passageway. There is a restaurant in the large open lobby on the second floor.

BANKS AND COMMERCIAL BUILDINGS

The original Colonial Bank (now the National Commercial Bank), Harbour Street, Kingston, Jamaica, was razed in the great fire of 1882, and a second building was partially destroyed twenty-five years later in the 1907 earthquake. The current neoclassical building was constructed in 1910. Its exterior features Tuscan columns and wrought-iron grillwork. The interior has a domed central ceiling and marble-faced pillars with Ionic capitals.

Banco de Credito y Ahorro, now Banco Santander, built in 1924, was the first bank in Ponce, Puerto Rico. Designed by Francisco Porrata Doria, the curved front of its corner facade is ornamented with two-story Corinthian engaged columns and pilasters. Broken pediments interrupt the balustraded roofline. The bank is famous for the spectacular art nouveau window over its entrance (see plate 64).

Banco de Ponce, designed by the same architect and built in the same year, is also a classically monumental building and is situated on a prominent triangular property. Tall, stylized Corinthian columns and pilasters provide a rhythm for the curved building's fenestration and support an entablature above which rises an attic story. A modestly scaled pedimented entrance occurs on the building axis.

Islamic influence, in combination with medieval, is apparent in much Spanish colonial architecture, but Havana, Cuba, also has good examples of later Islamic-revival work, among them two adjacent three-story buildings on Zulueta:

Fig. 423. Old picture postcard of the National Commercial Bank, 1910, Kingston, Jamaica, an example of eclectic neoclassicism

Fig. 424. Banco Santander, 1924, the first bank in Ponce, Puerto Rico

Palacio de las Ursulinas and Universal. Ursulinas, painted blue, uses different Islamic arched openings on each floor. The upper floor has horseshoe arches, each surrounded by a cinquefoil molding; the middle-level arches have trefoil heads; and the lower arcade employs interwoven multifoil arches. The yellow facade of Universal displays less Islamic variety than its neighbor. The small rectangular windows in the upper level are topped with trefoil blind arches, the two lower levels use multifoil pointed arches, and at the ground level diamond-geometry panels appear above these arches.

La Maderna Poesía is one of several art deco examples in Old Havana. This corner building is unadorned geometry, composed primarily of curved forms that are uninterrupted vertically. Horizontal emphasis occurs only above the corner entrance.

Buildings from five centuries are now neighbors in the historic section of Santo Domingo, Dominican Republic. One commercial building even displays carefully reproduced Sullivanesque ornament on its facade!

The position of McLaughlin Bank in Willemstad, Curaçao, provides part of the architectural containment of Wilhelmina Plaza. The building formerly housed the Freemasons. The red-tiled hip roof seems unrelated to the classical facade, which has a consistent theme of triangular pediments: one at the roofline that extends the entire dimension of the building, one on the Tuscan entrance portico, and those above each window. Classicism is further indicated in the quoins at the corners of the rectangular building.

Some of the most distinctive buildings in Charlotte Amalie, St. Thomas, U.S. Virgin Islands, are the mid-nineteenth-century warehouses lined up perpendic-

Fig. 425. Banco de Ponce, 1924, Ponce, Puerto Rico, classical monumentality

Fig. 426. Ursulinas, Havana, Cuba, with Islamic arcades

ular to the waterfront. The original arrangement was typically a double ware-house divided by a private work courtyard. These open work spaces and alleys have now become public walkways of active shopping malls, as the warehouses have been converted into sophisticated shops. Some of these shops have retained the bold brick arches and beamed ceilings of the original buildings.

On Kronprindsen, at Market Square, Charlotte Amalie, is the former St. Thomas Bank. The hip-roofed building is constructed of yellow brick laid in a striated pattern, with massive double doors in arched-head openings on the banking level. The most apparent architectural characteristic, however, is the two-level cast-iron colonnade fronting the building on its two street facades. Shops now occupy the lower level.

Fig. 427. Universal, Havana, Cuba, also with Islamic influence

Fig. 428. La Maderna Poesia, art deco in Havana, Cuba

Fig. 429. Sullivanesque ornament in Santo Domingo, Dominican Republic

Fig. 430. McLaughlin Bank, Willemstad, Curaçao

PUBLIC MARKETS

During the era of slavery, slaves were usually allowed to sell their excess produce at a Sunday market. The tradition of Sunday markets, usually now extended to include Saturday, has persisted in most Caribbean areas.

The first public market in Kingston, Jamaica, was Victoria Market, built in 1870 at the foot of King Street. Colorful produce crowded the stalls of this popular attraction every Sunday. The market was later relocated next to Victoria Pier and renamed Kingston Craft Market.

Vendue House, on Bay Street, was built about 1770, making it one of the oldest buildings in Nassau, Bahamas. It was originally a one-story open building with a roof supported by round columns. Once the scene of public auctions of slaves, cattle, and imported goods, about 1890 it was converted to house the head of the post office. Then it became a two-story building and was occupied by the Bahamas Electric Corporation. Now it is a museum of the history of the Bahamian slave trade. Elements of the original one-story building are evident: the arched openings, central pediment, rusticated masonry, and strong horizontal cornice.

Plaza del Marcado, in Ponce, Puerto Rico, was built in stages, its final expansion occurring in the 1930s. This enormous art deco market has been recently restored for use as an artisans' market.

The waterfront of Willemstad, Curaçao, is one of the most interesting areas of the town, particularly the Floating Market. Because of the lack of locally grown agricultural products, Curaçao depends heavily upon Venezuela for fruits and vegetables, which are sold from boats along the Willemstad waterfront. Brightly colored translucent "sails" provide shelter for the vendors and shoppers.

Fig. 431. Former St. Thomas Bank with two-level cast-iron colonnades, Charlotte Amalie, St. Thomas, U.S. Virgin Islands

Fig. 432. Old picture postcard, Victoria Market, 1870, the first public market in Kingston, Jamaica

Fig. 433. Old print of Vendue House, ca. 1770, one of the oldest buildings in Nassau, Bahamas

Fig. 434. Vendue House, now a museum of the history of the Bahamian slave trade

Market Square, at the west end of Main Street in Charlotte Amalie, St. Thomas, U.S. Virgin Islands, was the site of a notorious slave market, one of the busiest in the eighteenth century. It is now an active produce market on Saturday, when the townspeople congregate there to buy fresh fruits and vegetables. The current cast-iron structure came from a European railway company in the early 1900s.

Fig. 435. Plaza del Marcado, Ponce, Puerto Rico, recently restored art deco

Fig. 436. Entrance, Plaza del Marcado

Fig. 437. Floating Market, Willemstad, Curaçao, selling Venezuelan vegetables

Fig. 438. Market Square, Charlotte Amalie, St. Thomas, U.S. Virgin Islands, the site of an eighteenth-century slave market

TRANSPORTATION BUILDINGS

The Jamaican railway system can be traced to 1845, when a line ran from Kingston to Spanish Town, then the capital of Jamaica. The Kingston station was constructed on a grand scale, symbolizing the economic importance of this city as a center of trade. The station is brick, with prominent arcades on both levels of the east entrance end. The roof overhang on the track side was supported by Victorian cast-iron brackets.

Fig. 439. Old picture postcard, Railroad Station, 1845, Kingston, Jamaica; its scale indicated Kingston's economic importance

Fig. 440. Old Railroad Headquarters, 1924, Port of Spain, Trinidad, monumental eclecticism

Fig. 441. Railroad Station, Havana, Cuba, Spanish colonial-revival architecture

Fig. 442. Railroad Station, 1883, Matanzas, Cuba, in an un-Caribbean architectural style

The eclectic old Railroad Headquarters in Port of Spain, Trinidad, was built in 1924. Its main entrance combines an arch with a curved pediment and employs heavy rustications on the flanking columns and pilasters. The building is now the office of the Public Transport Service Corporation and Port of Spain Bus Terminal.

Railroads started operating in Cuba in 1837. The Havana Station is an interesting example of Spanish colonial-revival architecture. Built of brick, its facade has a rather severe symmetry with a central small but ornate pediment and twin square towers with Palladian openings at their tops.

An unexpected architectural style occurs in the railroad station at Matanzas, Cuba. Built in 1883, its steep roof and severe facade give no clue to its Caribbean location.

POTPOURRI

The Dome, Montego Bay, Jamaica, was built in 1837 for the purpose of sheltering the spring that for 200 years was the only reliable source of fresh water for the town. There is a charming legend about the origin of this spring. A little Spanish girl and her slave playmate were hunting crabs in this vicinity, and, upon moving a stone to find a crab, they heard the sound of bubbling water. They hurried to report this to their parents, who rushed to the site, dug, and found a spring. Delighted at having a new source of fresh water, the townspeople freed the little slave girl and built the Dome. After the end of the last century, the spring ceased to be the source of water for Montego Bay, but the Dome remains. Restored in 1976, it is two stories high, hexagonal in plan, with a crenellated parapet.

Phoenix Foundry, Falmouth, was one of the earliest industrial buildings in Jamaica and is the oldest in existence on the island. It was built about 1810 to make and repair machinery for sugar estates and for ships.

The bridge across the Rio Cobre in Spanish Town, Jamaica, was erected in 1801 and is the oldest iron bridge in the Western hemisphere. Designed by Thomas Wilson, it was prefabricated in Rotherham, Yorkshire, England, and shipped to Jamaica. Only a few examples of this bridge type, with small open-frame voussoirs, survive in the world today.

The Masonic Lodge is one of the oldest buildings in Bridgetown, Barbados,

Fig. 443. The Dome, 1837, once sheltered the water source for Montego Bay, Jamaica

Fig. 444. Phoenix Foundry, ca. 1810, Falmouth, Jamaica, the oldest existing industrial building on the island

and is listed by the Barbados National Trust. The stringcourse provides a strong horizontal emphasis, despite the building height and vertical alignment of the windows. The arches are different on each floor. This was the original home of Harrison College.

Christopher Columbus Cemetery, Havana, Cuba, occupies a fifty-six-acre site and was completed in 1871. It is laid out on the Roman camp concept, its four

Fig. 445. Bridge across the Rio Cobre, 1801, Spanish Town, Jamaica, the oldest iron bridge in the Western hemisphere

Fig. 446. Masonic Lodge, one of the oldest buildings in Bridgetown, Barbados, original home of Harrison College

Fig. 447. Christopher Columbus Cemetery, 1871, Havana, Cuba

Fig. 448. Cemetery chapel, Columbus Cemetery

quarters defined by major streets with a chapel located in a circle in the center. Each of the major quadrants is also subdivided into four parcels. There are four entrances, the major one, on the north, entitled "Gate of Peace." In the architecture of the mausoleums and small chapels is to be found every imaginable revival and eclectic style.

One of the Dominican Republic's most impressive small monuments is the

Fig. 449. Classical private chapel, Columbus Cemetery

Fig. 450. Altar of the Nation, Santo Domingo, the mausoleum of the three founding fathers of the Dominican Republic

Altar of the Nation, in Santo Domingo. Three heroic-size statues stand inside this white marble mausoleum, the three founding fathers of the Dominican Republic: Juan Pablo Duarte, Francisco del Rosario Sánchez, and Ramón Matías Mella. When the mausoleum was constructed, the remains of these three heroes were removed from the cathedral and placed in three niches here; above them burns an eternal flame.

GLOSSARY OF ARCHITECTURAL TERMS

Acroterion: Ornament at the corners or peak of a classical roof.

Ajoupa: Amerindian-type hut of mud and grass.

Antefixa: Ornament at the end of each row of roof tiles, also used to adorn the ridge of the roof.

Apse: Semicircular east termination of a church.

Arcade: Series of arches raised on columns or piers.

Architrave: Beam that rests directly on the column capital.

Art deco: Decorative style popular in the 1930s, employing curves and sharp angular or zigzag forms.

Art nouveau: Style popular toward the end of the nineteenth century, using organic and dynamic forms.

Ashlar: Hewn or squared building stone.

Balustrade: Railing system using short vertical members called balusters.

Bargeboard: Board at the termination of a projecting roof.

Baroque: Seventeenth-century European architectural style developing from late Renaissance and mannerism.

Barrel vault: Vault of semicircular cross-section.

Battlement: Parapet with repeated depressed openings through which missiles could be discharged.

Bond: The way in which masonry units are laid up.

Broken pediment: Pediment that has been broken apart at the center of its base or at its apex.

Buttress: Exterior mass of masonry used to provide resistance to lateral thrust.

Byzantine architecture: Fourth-century and later architecture of the Byzantine empire, exemplified by Hagia Sophia in Istanbul.

Capital: Topmost portion of a column or pilaster.

Caryatid: Sculptured human female figure acting as a column.

Castellation: *See* Battlement.

Chevet: Apse surrounded by an ambulatory that gives access to chapels.

Cinquefoil: Five-lobed design, the lobes separated by cusps.

Clapboard: Lapped horizontal wood siding, thicker along the lower edge.

Clasping buttress: Joining of two corner buttresses.

Clerestory: Row of windows in a church nave that rises above the side-aisle roof.

Colonnade: Row of columns supporting an entablature.

Comb: Uppermost ridge member on a roof.

Common bond: Brickwork exposing only stretchers, with staggered joints in alternate courses.

Composite order: Roman elaboration of Corinthian, combining volutes of the Ionic order.

Cooler: Boxlike projecting element offering a degree of privacy and sun protection at a window.

Coping: Protective top member of a wall, parapet, and so on.

Corbel: In masonry, a projection of the upper course or courses.

Corinthian order: Most ornate of the three Greek orders, featuring acanthus leaves in the capital.

Crenellation: *See* Battlement.

Cresting: Running ornament on the roof ridge.

Crowstep or corbie gable: Gable having a stepped edge.

Cupola: Small architectural element projecting above a roof, usually terminating in a small dome.

Demarara shutter: Louvered panel hinged at the top, located at a window.

Diagonal buttress: Buttress at a corner, positioned at forty-five degrees.

Dome: Rotated arch shape forming a curved roof structure.

Domical vault or coved vault: Four quarter-cylindrical convex surfaces that provide a domelike covering to a square area.

Doric order: Earliest and simplest of the three Greek orders.

Dormer: Window projecting vertically from a sloping roof.

Eclecticism: Combination of diverse architectural styles.

Engaged buttress: Exterior masonry mass bonded into a wall.

Engaged column: Column partially built into a wall.

English bond: Brickwork using alternate courses of headers and stretchers.

Entablature: In classical architecture, the horizontal member that spans columns, composed of the architrave, frieze, and cornice.

Facade: Exterior face of a building.

Fanlight: Semicircular or elliptical window above a door, with muntins radiating from the center.

Fascia: Edge member providing the finish closure of a roof projection.

Fenestration: Arrangement of windows in a building.

Finial: Ornament on the apex of a spire, gable, or pinnacle.

Flèche: Slender spire rising above a roof ridge. In French Gothic churches, the flèche frequently occurred over the intersection of the nave and transept roof ridges.

Flemish bond: In brickwork, each course consisting of headers and stretchers laid alternately.

Fluting: Vertical grooves cut into columns and pilasters.

Flying buttress: Buttress standing remote, receiving thrust from the building via a sloping or arched bar of masonry.

Foliated: Adorned with circular lobes or foils (trefoil, quatrefoil, cinquefoil, multifoil).

Fresco: Mural painted onto fresh plaster.

Fretwork: Ornamental open woodwork, usually cut with a scroll saw.

Gable roof: Double-sloping roof with triangular portions at the end walls of the building.

Gallery: Long covered area on the exterior of a building.

Gambrel roof: Similar to a gable roof but with two slopes on each side, a steeper pitch occurring on the lower roof section.

Garland: Ornamental festoon of leaves, flowers, or fruit.

Georgian architecture: Prevailing eighteenth-century architectural style in Great Britain and its colonies, named after the first three Georges and derived from classical, Renaissance, and baroque.

Gothic arch: Pointed arch.

Gothic architecture: Style derived from Romanesque and Byzantine during the later twelfth century, intent upon achieving greater building height. Uses pointed arches, flying buttresses, and greater areas of stained glass.

Great house: Home of the plantation or estate owner.

Greek cross: Cross with four arms of equal dimension.

Groin: Curved line formed by the intersection of the surfaces of two vaults.

Half-timbered: Exposed timber structures with masonry infill between the wood members.

Hall church: Church with nave and side aisles but without clerestories admitting light directly to the nave.

Hammerbeam: Bracketed horizontal member protruding from the wall, supporting a trussed roof system.

Header: Masonry unit laid up with its end exposed.

Hip roof: Roof that slopes up from all four sides.

Horseshoe arch: Arch whose curve is somewhat greater than a semicircle, making its opening at the bottom less than its greatest span.

In antis: Columns set between projecting walls.

Ionic order: Greek classical order characterized primarily by the volutes of its column capitals.

Jacobean architecture: Early-seventeenth-century English architectural style named after James I, incorporating the curvilinear gable and various continental Renaissance influences.

Jalousies: Operable window louvers of various materials.

Latin cross: Cross with the upright arm much longer than the crossarm.

Latticework: Crossing of thin strips of material as in a trellis, usually in a diagonal pattern.

Lintel: Horizontal structural member over an opening.

Machicolations: Openings in a projecting element at the parapet of a fortified building, through which pitch, boiling water, and stones could be thrown down upon the enemy.

Mansard roof: Roof with a double slope on all four sides, the lower slope (as in the gambrel) being much steeper.

Medieval architecture: Architecture occurring from approximately the fifth to the fifteenth centuries, including Byzantine, Romanesque, and Gothic styles.

Metope: In the Doric frieze, the space between the triglyphs.

Minaret: Tall tower adjacent to a mosque from which the faithful are called to prayer.

Moorish architecture: Architecture occurring in areas under Islamic control, including portions of Spain and North Africa.

Mosaic: Surface decoration using small pieces of stone, tile, or glass to form a pattern.

Mudéjar style: Islamic style created in Spain during the thirteenth and fourteenth centuries by Moors, even though the area was dominated by Christianity at that time.

Multifoil: Composition having more than five foils or lobes.

Nogging: Similar to half-timbering.

Parapet: Wall extension above the roof.

Pavilion: An element on a facade, usually central or terminal, made prominent by plan projection, height, and so on.

Pediment: In classical architecture, the triangular gable above the horizontal cornice; later also used over doors and windows, and sometimes curved or broken.

Pendentives: Spherical triangular forms that make the transition between a circular element (dome or drum) and a square support system (usually composed of four columns or piers).

Pepperbox turret: Circular turret with a conical or domical roof.

Pierced gable: In a protrusion above the roof, a gable with openings that frequently housed bells.

Pilaster: Rectangular pier incorporated into a wall.

Pinnacle: Protruding small ornamental element, frequently placed atop buttresses, at the corners of towers, and so on.

Polychrome: Varicolored.

Portico: Porch.

Prairie style: Architectural characteristics popularized by Frank Lloyd Wright, including horizontal emphasis and generous roof overhangs.

Quadripartite vault: Groined vault over a rectangular area, divided into four parts by intersecting diagonals.

Quatrefoil: Four-lobed pattern.

Quoins: Elements at the corner of a building that structurally reinforce that area; also usually provide decorative distinction by being of a contrasting material.

Reja: Wood or metal grill covering a building opening.

Renaissance architecture: Style that originated in fifteenth-century Italy and succeeded Gothic as the popular style all over Europe.

Ribs: Moldings that project from the surface to provide strength or design emphasis, such as at the groins of intersecting vaults.

Ridge: Horizontal line where two sloping roof surfaces meet.

Rococo: A decorative architectural style that developed in France around the middle of the eighteenth century and replaced baroque; it had only partial acceptance in other parts of Europe.

Romanesque architecture: Style that emerged in the early eleventh century based on Roman and Byzantine concepts; its experimentation with vault construction led to the eventual development of Gothic.

Rose window: Large circular stained-glass window, usually with tracery in a radial pattern.

Rubble: Rough stones of irregular sizes and shapes.

Rustication: Coarse-textured stone with emphasized joints.

Segmental arch: Arch using less than a semicircle.

Sexpartite vault: Intersection of three vaulted surfaces, producing six triangular surfaces per bay.

Single house: One-room-deep arrangement with the rooms in a row perpendicular to the street, accessed from a gallery along one side.

Spire: Slender termination of a steeple, generally an octagonal pyramid.

Steeple: Series of stories atop a building or tower, the elements diminishing in size and topped by a spire.

Stretcher: Masonry unit laid up with its long dimension exposed.

Stringcourse: Horizontal band extending across the facade of a building.

Stucco: Exterior finish composed of cement, lime, and sand mixed with water.

Sullivanesque: In the manner of Louis Sullivan, turn-of-the-century U.S. architect, whose buildings displayed sensitive organic decoration.

Thatch: Technique used most frequently for roofing, including a variety of materials such as palm fronds, straw, reeds, or grass.

Transept: Transverse portion of a church plan that crosses the main axis, producing a cruciform shape.

Transom: Glazed panel above a door.

Trefoil: Three-lobed pattern.

Triglyph: In a Doric frieze, the panel composed of three vertical bands that occurs between the metopes.

Tripartite roof: Three-part roof, usually with three gables expressed on the facade.

Trompe l'oeil: Deceptively real painting.

Turret: Small tower, usually corbeled from a building corner.

Tuscan order: Simplest of the Roman orders, patterned after Doric.

Tympanum: Segmental or triangular surface enclosed by an arch or pediment, usually above a wall opening.

Vault: In its simplest form, an extended arch.

Vergeboard: Bargeboard.

Veranda: Open gallery or porch.

Victorian architecture: Nineteenth-century expression of revival and eclectic architecture in Great Britain and its colonies, named after the reign of Queen Victoria.

Volute: Spiral scroll used on the Ionic capital.

Watertable: Projecting horizontal masonry element indicating the transition between the foundation wall and the upper wall.

Wattle and daub: Primitive construction technique in which a woven basketwork of saplings, branches, vines, or split bamboo is coated with mud plaster.

Wheel window: Rose window.

BIBLIOGRAPHY

Acworth, A. W. *Buildings of Architectural or Historic Interest in the British West Indies.* New York: Johnson Reprint Corporation, 1970.

Adkins, Leonard M. *A Walking Guide to the Caribbean.* Boulder, Colo.: Johnson, 1988.

Besson, Gerard. *A Photographic Album of Trinidad at the Turn of the Nineteenth Century.* Port of Spain, Trinidad: Paria, 1985.

Berthelot, Jack, and Martine Gaumé. *Kaz Antiye.* Guadeloupe: Editions Perspectives Creoles, 1983.

Buisseret, David. *Historic Architecture of the Caribbean.* London: Heinemann, 1980.

Douglas, Robert. *Island Heritage: Architecture of the Bahamas.* Nassau: Darkstream, 1992.

Dyde, Brian. *Islands to the Windward.* London and Basingstoke: Macmillan, 1987.

Ellis, G. *Saint Lucia—Helen of the West Indies.* 2d ed. London and Basingstoke: Macmillan, 1988.

Fermor, P. L. *The Traveller's Tree.* London: Penguin, 1984.

Franciscus, J. A. *Haiti—Voodoo Kingdom to Modern Riviera.* San Juan: Franciscus Family Foundation, 1980.

Fraser, Henry, and Ronnie Hughes. *Historic Houses of Barbados.* 2d ed. Bridgetown, Barbados: Barbados National Trust and Art Heritage, 1986.

Gjessing, F. C., and W. P. MacLean. *Historic Buildings of St. Thomas and St. John.* London: Macmillan, 1987.

Hannau, Hans W. *The West Indian Islands.* Miami: Argos, n.d.

Higman, B. W. *Jamaica Surveyed.* Kingston, Jamaica: Institute of Jamaica, 1988.

Hill, Barbara. *Historic Churches of Barbados.* Bridgetown, Barbados: Art Heritage, 1984.

Hoyos, F. A. *Barbados—The Visitor's Guide.* London and Basingstoke: Macmillan, 1983.

Innis, Probyn. *Historic Basseterre—The Story of a West Indian Town.* St. John's, Antigua: Antigua Printing and Publishing, 1985.

Jesse, Charles. *Outlines of St. Lucia's History.* 4th ed. Castries, St. Lucia: St. Lucia Archaeological and Historical Society, 1986.

Jopling, C. F. *Puerto Rican Houses in Sociohistorical Perspective.* Knoxville: University of Tennessee Press.

Lewis, J. N. *Architecture of the Caribbean.* New York: American Institute of Architects Service, 1984.

Peggs, A. D. *A Short History of the Bahamas.* 3d ed. Nassau: Nassau Daily Tribune, 1959.

Russell, C. S. *Nassau's Historic Buildings.* Nassau: Bahamas National Trust, 1979.

Saunders, Gail. *The Bahamas—A Family of Islands.* London: Macmillan, 1988.

Sinclair, Norma. *Grenada, Isle of Spice.* London and Basingstoke: Macmillan, 1988.

Slesin, Susan, Stafford Cliff, Jack Berthelot, et al. *Caribbean Style.* New York: Clarkson N. Potter, 1985.

Upton, Dill, ed. *America's Architectural Roots.* Washington, D.C.: Preservation Press, 1986.

Watterson, G. G. *This Old House.* Newtown, Trinidad: Paria, 1988.

INDEX

Abarca, Silvestre, 147
adaptive use of historic buildings
—as archives, museums, galleries: from an arsenal, 147; from a barracks, 141; from a church, 198, 213; from a courthouse, 162; from a fort, 147, 154, 155; from a government building, 171; from a market, 232; from a prison, 141; from a residence, 89, 104, 113, 115, 125
—as hotels, guest houses, apartments: from a barracks, 138; from a convent, 198; from a dockyard facility, 137; from a fort, 154; from a hospital, 141; from a residence, 77, 96, 101, 106, 111, 119, 130
—as libraries, 128, 166
—as a mausoleum, 203
—as office space: from a barracks, 138; from a convent, 198, 202; from a fort, 141, 152; from a hotel, 223, 229; from a military building, 147; from a residence, 117, 125
—as a post office, 180
—as restaurants: from a dockyard facility, 137; from a fort, 152; from a residence, 74, 78, 96, 99, 111, 115, 117
—as retail spaces: from a bank, 231; from a customs office, 179; from a dockyard facility, 137; from a fort, 152; from a hotel, 229; from a slave-holding area, 19; from a warehouse, 231
—as schools: from a barracks, 138, 143; from a capitol, 171; from a fort, 135; from a gunpowder magazine, 147; from a hotel, 222; from an insane asylum, 169; from a residence, 74
—as social/recreational facilities, 141, 213, 225
adoquines, 31
African influence, 58, 59, 66
Almirall, Raymond F., 183
Amerindians, 6, 8. *See also* Arawak Indians; Carib Indians; Siboney Indians
Antigua: Admiral's House, 104; background and urbanization, 18, 19; Clarence House, 103; earthquakes, 188; English Harbour, 137; Fort James, 136; military facilities, 136–38; museum, 11; Nelson's Dockyard, 137; public and institutional buildings, 162; religious buildings, 188; Shirley Heights, 137; Weatherhills great house, 103
—residences: large, 103–4; medium, 78; small, 63
—St. John's, 19; Cathedral of St. John the Divine, 19, 188; Courthouse (Antigua and Barbuda Archives), 162; Redcliffe Quay, 19; St. Joseph's Church, 188

Antilles, 1
Antillia, 1
Antonelli, Juan Bautista, 147
Arawak Indians: in Cuba, 32; in Curaçao, 46; encountered by Columbus, 8–9; in Hispaniola, 35; Igneri, 9; Lucayo, 9; in Puerto Rico, 30, 67; residences of (*ajoupas, canayes, carbets*), 10, 11; Sevilla la Nueva site, Jamaica, 12; Taíno, 9, 32, 67; use of thatch by, 59; U.S. Virgin Islands, 48; White Marl site, Jamaica, 11
art deco, 220, 221, 224, 230, 232
art nouveau, 229

Bacon, John, 156
Bahamas: background and urbanization, 26–29; Charles Towne (Nassau), 26–27; Guanahani (San Salvador), 26; military facilities, 143–44; public and institutional buildings, 166–68; religious buildings, 194–96. *See also* Nassau
—Grant's Town, 66; St. Agnes' Parish Church, 195
—residences: large, 109–11; medium, 83–84; small, 66
Barbados: background and urbanization, 20–22; Barbadian parapet, 80; Codrington College, 218–19; Drax Hall Plantation, 105–6; Marine Hotel, Hastings, 223; military facilities, 140–41; museum, 141; public and institutional buildings, 163–64; religious buildings, 189–91; St. Ann's Fort, 140; St. Matthias, Hastings, 189; St. Nicholas Abbey, 105; Sam Lord's Castle, 106; Savannah, 141; Villa Franca, Hastings, 80; Villa Nova, 107. *See also* Bridgetown
—residences: large, 105–7; medium, 78–80; small, 64
Barre, Jemro, 150
Basseterre, St. Kitts: the Circus, 16; Co-Cathedral of the Immaculate Conception, 187; Georgian House Restaurant, 78; Independence Square (Pall Mall Square), 17; Presbytery, 78; St. George's Parish Church, 187; Treasury Building, 161–62; Warner Park, 18; Wesley Methodist Church, 187; Zion Moravian Church, 187
Battle of the Saints, 156
Battle of Waterloo, 138
Baussan, Georges, 150, 174
Beese, Henri, 150
Black River. *See* Jamaica
Bligh, Capt. William, 152, 211
bohío, 67–68